Virginia Satir:
Foundational Ideas

Virginia Satir: Foundational Ideas

Barbara Jo Brothers
Editor

Tulane School of Social Work

Routledge
Taylor & Francis Group
New York London

Virginia Satir: Foundational Ideas has also been published as *Journal of Couples Therapy*, Volume 2, Numbers 1/2 1991.

Routledge is an imprint of the Taylor & Francis Group, an informa business

First issued in paperback 2016

First published by:

The Haworth Press, Inc. 10 Alice Street, Binghamton, NY 13904-1580
EUROSPAN/Haworth, 3 Henrietta Street, London WC2E 8LU England

This edition published 2011 by Routledge:

Routledge
Taylor & Francis Group
711 Third Avenue
New York, NY 10017

Routledge
Taylor & Francis Group
27 Church Road
Hove East Sussex BN3 2FA

Library of Congress Cataloging-in-Publication Data

Virginia Satir : foundational ideas / Barbara Jo Brothers, editor.
    p. cm.
    ISBN 1-56024-104-7 (alk. paper)
    1. Family psychotherapy. 2. Marital psychotherapy. 3. Satir, Virginia. I. Brothers, Barbara, 1937- .
RC488.5.V55   1991
616.89'156 – dc20   90-26287
                                                                                        CIP

ISBN13: 978-1-56024-104-1 (hbk)
ISBN13: 978-1-138-99407-2 (pbk)

Virginia Satir: Foundational Ideas

CONTENTS

ABOUT THE EDITOR

Barbara Jo Brothers, MSW, BCD, a Diplomate in Clinical Social Work, National Association of Social Workers, is in private practice in New Orleans. She received her BA from the University of Texas and her MSW from Tulane University, where she is currently on the faculty. She was editor of *The Newsletter of the American Academy of Psychotherapists* from 1976 to 1985, and was associate editor of *Voices: The Art and Science of Psychotherapy* from 1979 to 1989. She has had nearly 30 years of experience, in both the public and private sectors, helping people to form skills that will enable them to connect emotionally. The author of numerous articles and book chapters on authenticity in human relating, she has advocated healthy, congruent communication that builds intimacy as opposed to destructive, incongruent communication which blocks intimacy. In addition to her many years of direct work with couples and families, Ms. Brothers has led numerous workshops on teaching communication in families and has also played an integral role in the development of training programs in family therapy for mental health workers throughout the Louisiana state mental health system.

Introduction

Barbara Jo Brothers

. . . Amid these [world] changes is the growing conviction that human beings must evolve a new consciousness that place a high value on being human, that leads toward cooperation, that enables positive conflict resolution and that recognizes our spiritual foundations. Can we accept as a given that the self of the therapist is an essential factor in the therapeutic process? If this turns out to be true, it will alter our way of teaching therapists as well as treating patients. (Satir, 1987, pg. 25).

VIRGINIA: THE WORK

This volume is dedicated to the late and lovely Virginia Satir, mentor to many and enigma to others in the world of family therapy. The legacy left by Virginia,[1] *this* very exceptional being, includes her profound insight into the behaviour of human beings and the guidelines for the application of universal principles in such a way as to enhance human growth and unite individuals.

During the year after her death, there were beautiful tributes made to Virginia Satir which focused on her life from a personal point of view. *This* tribute—while fully recognizing her position that the personal cannot effectively be separated from the treatment process—focuses on her *ideas* and *thinking;* it was very important to Virginia that her work be understood as teachable and learnable. Presented are her ideas and her major processes, the processes having been designed as vehicles to facilitate the training of the self that would be therapist. The articles in this collection reflect her most basic ideas about the healing quality of respect for all people and the emphasis on the person of both therapist and patient—as opposed to

1

the emphasis on technique. All the contributors in these pages had personal contact with Virginia. Those who describe her theories and processes had extensive contact with her, were the mentored; they knew, loved, and worked very closely with Virginia over a number of years. Thus, this collection represents an excellent sample of her work (— in so far as her so very experiential work *can* be captured on the printed page. The serious student might want to supplement this reading with the viewing of videotapes of Virginia working and by enrolling in a training seminar that teaches the Satir system). The masterly work of Virginia, the mentor, shines through.

The roots of the previously mentioned enigmatic factor may also become more clear through reading this collection. This enigmatic factor was born of Virginia's very exceptional breadth and depth of *view* as well as of spirit; it will be addressed in the next section of this introduction — VIRGINIA: THE VISIONARY. To be able to see — to perceive — more than does the average person is both the gift and the burden of the brilliant. The uniqueness of Virginia's genius lay in the fact that she *was* able to translate her larger vision for the therapist who attended her longer training programs. Her "magic" demonstrated in a weekend workshop was composed, again, of those teachable, learnable skills; the thirteen contributors to this volume are living testimony to that fact.

In this issue are the assorted representative pictures of Virginia's work. Those pictures present her foundational ideas: her triad concept, her model for change, her communication theory, her parts party process, her family reconstruction process, her temperature reading process, and her belief in the worth of the person. Maxine West and Bala Jaison also show examples of directions in which her work may be expanded and synthesized with the work of others.

Yetta Bernhard provides an excellent summary of Virginia's therapeutic activity; what she did and why she did it. She cogently describes Virginia's basic theses and methods. Michele Baldwin, who co-authored with Virginia, *Step-By-Step*, presents one view of the triad concept — the basic unit of humankind. Virginia has said that coupling will go as parenting went. Michele describes "Charlie's" process of data-gathering in his experience in his first triad, his family of origin. Charlie will grow up to be half of a pair or to spend energy *avoiding* being half of a pair, based on those early learnings. Judith Bula Jacobs goes on to explain how any "Charlie's " experience in "triad-ing" will influence his experience in coupling.

Joan E. Winter and Leanne R. E. Parker describe how marital relationships may be enhanced through the Parts Party, Virginia's way of bringing to vibrant life the integration of the many-hued aspects of the self. Walter F. Zahnd and Lynne M. Azpeitia have extended her group temperature reading vehicle to use in the coupling process.

Laura Sue Dodson has contributed an in-depth presentation of Virginia's model for change, what Virginia considered the components in the change process and how change in the individual extends out to change in the couple, in the family, into the greater community and, thence into the world. William Nerin has spelled out, in detail, the theory behind family reconstruction. This process was developed by Virginia in the early sixties to provide a means for going, with the patient, back through their past to find—then free them from—their old learnings. Michael D. Spiegler speaks to Virginia's deep conviction about the essential goodness at the core of the human being as the secret to her success with the toughest of clients—who Virginia always measured in terms of degree of the depths of their pain rather than degree of difficulty. Spiegler speaks of that deep conviction as the energy behind her "endurance" in working with the difficult.

Jaison discusses the points where Virginia's work interfaces with Focusing, developed by Eugene Gendlin. She also provides evidence from personal experience of Speigler's point of the value of Virginia's "everybody is a wonderful human being " attitude. She relates a personal example of the impact and operational value of that philosophy on the specific human being. Jaison goes on to demonstrate Virginia's own description of her work as containing terms more spiritual than clinical, citing this as a possible point of departure from the general run of family therapists.

Birgitte Winkel of Denmark writes of the impact of her exposure, early in her career, to Virginia's work. Winkel's article is one example of the hundreds of lives Virginia touched around the world. Maxine West's work on shame-based identity was inspired by Virginia. West sees the shame-based identity as being on the opposite end of a continuum from an identity based on self esteem, presenting another good example of how Virginia's ideas can be extended and applied. Her article provides further evidence of the value of the concept of the relationship between nurturing/healing/wholing and self-esteem.

Laura Sue Dodson and I give our different perspectives on Virginia's dying process, Laura Sue focusing on the last week or so of Virginia's life. "Healing Virginia" is a focus on the period of time during which Virginia was still mobilizing her energy toward continued living in this dimension, the living world as we know it. In conclusion, Lynne M. Azpeitia has provided a thorough bibliography, including videotapes, which will be very helpful for those who want to study Virginia's work.

VIRGINIA: THE VISIONARY

Virginia was able to manifest and to *teach the manifestations* of philosophies taught by venerated thinkers and philosophers stretching out, through time, behind her. She designed processes which made available the experiencing of the Tao, of Teilhard's ultra-human, of Gandhi's *ahimsa* [truth-force]. If they were the theory, Virginia was the laboratory experience.

Virginia knew how to bring the spiritual experience into right-now time between two ordinary human beings; she could teach the process so that they might later do it "on their own time."

Having spent considerable time in Virginia's company on both a personal and professional basis, I would like to share my perspective on how the one (personal) shades into the other (professional): Virginia's profession *was* the implementation and enhancement of her person and that of the person with whom she encountered at any given moment in time. She believed rigid distinctions between personal behavior and professional behavior could be both a strategic and a moral therapeutic error. Being a *person*, for her, was as high a calling as was being a professional. Experiencing full personhood in interaction with another person doing the same is, in Virginia's definition, a spiritual experience. Seeking to implement such basic truth of experience on a world-wide basis is the mark of the great visionary.

On personhood and therapy, she says:

> I have learned that when I am fully present with the patient or family, I can move therapeutically with much greater ease. I can simultaneously reach the depths to which I need to go, and at the same time honor the fragility, the power and the *sacredness of life* [italics mine] in the other. When I am in touch with myself, my feelings, my thoughts, with what I see and hear, I am growing toward becoming a more integrated self. I am more congruent, I am more 'whole,' and I am able to make greater contact with the other person . . . . In a nutshell, what I have been describing are therapists who put their personhood and that of their patients first. (Satir, 1987, pg. 23)

Being "fully present with the patient" requires being in the here and now. "Congruence," in the sense in which Virginia used it, is always a "now" experience. To speak to working in the "now," the "given time," I search through my metaphor stock, knowing such a present-focused activity is not easily captured in description. Quicker than humming birds, faster than lightening flashes, "now" is always finished with the very sound of the word leaving the mouth. As recognition of *feelings* is essential to the process of human beingness, Virginia's work was with the Now and the Flow of the Now.

> And affect is always now. You cannot feel now for yesterday. What you do now when you think of yesterday is feel now the *memory* you have of yesterday. You cannot feel the feel of tomorrow today unless you make a fantasy or an expectation, and that brings to you today, but that [tomorrow] isn't present [today]. So your *affect* is always now. (Banmen and Satir, 1983, pg. 125).

Virginia's necessary focus on the "here and now," integral to congruence, is essential to potentiate the healing properties of congruence — the harmonic convergence, in the now, of body, mind, feelings, facial expression, and verbal expressions. Her keen observation of the relationship between that crucial congruence and self esteem was at the heart of her work; the *healing energy thus freed* was considered, by her, to be a spiritual experience.

This vital work with the Now and the Flow of the Now sounds very similar to the very ancient Chinese Taoism. I have described Virginia's philosophy as fitting very well with that of Lao Tzu (1989). Her concept of keeping to the Flow of Life seems synonymous with the concept of the Tao, here translated "Truth."

> Truth [Tao] is the name given to that which was originally nameless and simple. Though small, the whole world cannot subjugate it. When the rulers abide by it, all animate creation will of their own accord become their servants. Because heaven and earth are one with Truth [Tao], they produce rains and dews which benefit all mankind without their asking. Truth [Tao] is to the universe as rivers and seas are to the earth. (Chen Lin, 1965, p. 98)

Like the ancient Chinese philosophers, Virginia also understood all of Life as connected:

> We're in the river, the river of life that surrounds us all the time. So here we come up and we bubble and others come up and they bubble and we move and so on. And then that idea of being one in Life becomes very important. We have just begun to introduce spirituality into human relations. (Satir, 1987a, tape 4)

Virginia took the concept of Truth — actualized as congruence — observed thousands of human beings across the earth, and applied the unifying quality inherent in the nature of Truth to human interaction, never losing sight of "the energy that comes from the fact that we are all part of the Life Force" (1987a, tape 5). It was Virginia's experience that "the connectedness of all of you can only enhance your own energy" (1987a, tape 5).

This human connectedness of being one in Life which Virginia could mobilize in her training groups, speaks to Pierre Teilhard's vision of a new and un-named energy possible in humankind. I hear echoes back and forth between her ideas and his.

Teilhard de Chardin:

> Every day the reality of an ultra-human becomes more insistent; and there is no possible way for our generation to enter into it except with the help of a new form of psychic energy in which the personalizing depth of love is combined with the totalization of what is most essential and most universal in the heart of the stuff of the cosmos and the cosmic stream — and for this new energy we have as yet *no name*! (1963, pg. 227)

Virginia (from a meditation):

> And now let yourself again come in touch with being a child of the universe . . . of feeling the sense of life-force that is in all that is around you: the plants, the animals, the people, the grasses, the sky the trees.
>
> And as these two energies meet, the energies of inspiration and the energy of groundedness, creating still *a third energy* [italics mine], the energy of connectedness to other beings, human beings. (Satir, 1983, pg. 102).

This "new energy," perhaps this "third energy," for which we have as yet "no name," is born in the nurturing environs created by that mutual exchange, between two human beings, of truth — distilled by Virginia to congruent communication. Virginia took Truth, applied it directly to the human beings before her and created Teilhard's "personalizing depth of love" within the tangible, breathing family unit. As much philosopher as therapist, this depth and breadth of scope may explain why she is not more widely understood.

The world trembled a little when Virginia died — the therapy world acknowledged her in a ripple around the planet. We all stood an honor guard at her passage . . .

Sheldrake, himself trying to illustrate a new paradigm, shakes me into another view of the essence of her legacy in his discussion of Thomas Kuhn's concept of paradigm from Kuhn's book, *The Structure of Scientific Revolution*.

'A paradigm is what the members of a scientific community share, *and*, conversely, a scientific community consists of men who share a paradigm.' Kuhn argues that normal science is a cumulative and progressive activity that consists of solving puzzles within the context of shared paradigm; but that scientific revolutions, which are extraordinary and relatively infrequent, involve the establishment of a new paradigm or framework. Typically, this does not, at least at first, makes sense to practitioners brought up within the old paradigm; a period of controversy ensues, which ends only when existing professionals have either been converted to the new paradigm or have died off and been replaced by a new generation familiar with it. (Sheldrake 1988, pg. 265-266)

That was the unsettling factor, the phenomenon that brought the uneasiness to the family therapy community in the early seventies when the discipline of family therapy was still trying to form identity. She described a new, more encompassing border where one had so recently been formed. Who was ready yet to pull up the stakes and stick them out so far? Had we not just got them in the ground good? Even as family therapy was evolving, Virginia was pulling it along into its expanded version — all the lesser ones of us running along behind struggling to keep up. We had just succeeded in getting all the *family members* into the office, Virginia, what did you mean the *world*?!

There were those in the family therapy world who thought she had diverged from the discipline of psychotherapy with families; in fact, she had expanded the definition. Lynn Hoffman hinted at this direction in her address, in New Orleans a few weeks after Virginia's death in 1988, to the American Association of Marriage and Family Therapy. She said the organization could not contain such a great soul as Virginia; she was bigger than us all.

Virginia and Teilhard and Lao Tzu with the larger vision — with the deep seeing vision — could see the Oneness, the unity groping to form.

Virginia Satir had much more in common with men like Gandhi than she ever had with whoever might be the current president of whatever association of psychotherapists.

Reflecting much of Virginia's basic philosophy, Gandhi says:

> Man and his deed are two distinct things. Whereas a good deed
> should call forth approbation and a wicked deed disapproba-
> tion, the doer of the deed, whether good or wicked, always
> deserves respect or pity as the case may be. 'Hate the sin and
> not the sinner' is a precept which, though easy enough to un-
> derstand, is rarely practiced, and that is why the poison of
> hatred spreads in the world.
> This *ahimsa* ["truth-force"] is the basis of the search for
> truth. I am realizing every day that the search is vain unless it
> is founded on *ahimsa* as the basis. It is quite proper to resist
> and attack a system, but to resist and attack its author is tanta-
> mount to resisting and attacking oneself. For we are all tarred
> with the same brush, and are children of one and the same
> Creator, and as such the divine powers within us are infinite.
> To slight a single human being is to slight those divine powers,
> and thus to harm not only that being but with him the whole
> world. (Gandhi, 1957, pg. 276)

Virginia says:

> So often we mistakenly think that what is bad and wrong is
> inside and are not aware this is a behavioral description, not an
> identity. (1987, Tape 1)

> . . . the more you appreciate yourself, the less you will have to
> depreciate any one else. Put another way, the more you can
> appreciate yourself, the more you can appreciate others.
> (1986, Tape 1)

People like Virginia and Gandhi were about paradigm shifting.
Both envisioned literal changes in the world as a result of their
work. Part of the reason Virginia did not take the time to write the
books we now wish were written is because she saw herself as *doing* the needed work. Each person given the awareness of their own
worth was another force in the world for removing the pain of that
kind of hunger from the world. It was as if we were all candles and
a certain number of us must first be lit in order for there to be
sufficient light to see the Whole.

The family is a microcosm. By knowing how to heal the family, I know how to heal the world. Virginia Satir (Laign, 1988, p. 20)

Although imminently practical in her application, Virginia was a spiritual giant in our time, spending most of her life in providing *experiences* that held the lessons she taught . . . . And it appears she had her fingertips on the very Pulse of Life.

NOTE

1. Virginia Satir is remembered as having stated her dislike for hearing herself referred to as a "Satir." For this reason, there is some departure, in these pages, from that customary formality of scholarly presentations.

REFERENCES

Brothers, B.J. (1989). Virginia Satir and Lao Tzu: a new look at ancient wisdom. *Voices: The Art and Science of Psychotherapy, 25*(1&2), 105-113.

Chen Lin Kuo (1969). *Truth and nature*. Hong Kong: Wan Ku Shu Tien.

Laign, J. (1988, Oct/Nov.) Healing human spirits, creating joy in living. Interview with Virginia Satir. *Focus on chemically dependent families, 11*(5), 20-21, 28-32.

Gandhi, M. (1957). *Gandhi: an autobiography. The story of my experiments with truth*. Boston: Beacon Paperback Edition.

Satir, V.(1987). The therapist story. *Journal of Psychotherapy and the Family, 3*(1), 17-25.

Satir, V. (Speaker). (1987a). Avanta Process Community VII, module I, (cassette recordings #4 & 5). Crested Butte, Colorado: Blue Moon Cassettes.

Satir, V., & Banmen, J. (1983). *Virginia Satir: process community III 1983*. (Available from J. Banmen, Delta Psychological Associates, Inc., 11213 Canyon Crescent, North Delta, British Columbia, Canada, V4E 2R6.)

Satir, V. & Baldwin, M. (1983). *Satir step by step*. Palo Alto, California: Science and Behavior Books.

Sheldrake R. (1988). *The presence of the past*. New York: Vintage Books.

Teilhard, P. (1963). *Activation of energy*. New York: Harcourt Brace Jovanovich, Inc.

Methods for Connectedness:
Virginia Satir's Contribution
to the Process
of Human Communication

Barbara Jo Brothers

So at this moment, seeing yourself becoming ever more *congruent*, ever more aware of you as a choice maker and as a manifestation of Life. And letting yourself be reminded that as beings of the universe we are connected to the energy from the center of the earth . . . Now let yourself go to the center of the earth . . . wherein continual energy is always present . . . and let yourself be that energy from the center of the earth, moving upward into your feet and legs . . . giving you your grounding, the energy of your grounding . . . keeping yourself in touch with the earth. . . . feeling that energy move slowly, comfortably upward through you feet and legs . . . Now let yourself become aware of the energy from the heavens . . . as that energy moves down through your head and through your body from the top . . . The energy of your inspiration . . . of your imagination, of your sensing, of your creativity. And as those two energies move together, again rhythmically, groundedly . . . As they meet they create a third energy, *the energy of your connectedness with other people* [italics added], a third energy, *that which comes as we really recognize our worth* [italics added], standing on our own feet and moving out to people outside ourselves . . . that can move out through your arms and hands, and sometimes in your skin, and touch other people. A clean, tingling of energy from groundedness, for inspiration and imagination and intuition, for your ability *to be con-*

11

nected to other people [italics added]. And remind yourself
that those energies are always there . . . that it's only a matter
of how you tune into that. They never stop, no more than the
sun stops shining somewhere in the world . . . Now let your
attention move to that place deep inside yourself, where you
keep *the treasure that is called by your name* [italics added]
. . . And as you move there, again to notice what you have . . .
your ability to see, to hear, to taste and smell, to speak, to
think and feel, to move and to choose. They all came with you
with your package . . . And again, those are always there, and
you need only to tune into them and know how to use them for
you. Now again, be in touch with your breathing . . . Perhaps
you can again begin to feel the wonder that you are, the miracle that is us . . . Perhaps you can be aware of how carefully
we take care of our treasure, how carefully you take care of
your treasure . . . Let your own being and your own self become whatever treasures . . . (Satir, 1982, pg. 19-20)

This is a portion of one of Virginia's "meditations" or what she
called "a way of bringing our energy so we can focus . . . because
we have so many parts, with energy moving in all kinds of ways"
(1982, pg. 2). It contains basic elements of her healing "magic,"
that which she sought to render comprehensible to as many human
beings as possible. The only way to enter into the feeling aspect of
that kind of learning experience is to participate in the meditation in
some way; I seek here to enter into the *cognitive* aspect, recognizing
the artificiality of the distinction.

Like sunrise and the break of day, this third energy of *"connectedness"* seems to be so ordinary an occurrence that we do not stop
and take conscious note of its magnificence. It is the awareness that
does make all the difference. Virginia sought to bring the awareness.

There are profound psychobiological and sociological implications from and for the particular five patterns of communication
Virginia observed and delineated during her 51 years of professional work, watching interaction after interaction, with thousands
of families across the globe. From *thousands* of families over all
those years, observed by one of the keenest eyes of the psychothera-

peutic world. Virginia sorted out the components of what makes that "connectedness" possible. She experienced and presented that "third energy" as a dynamic living force and nurtured the living flame of it wherever she found it.

Virginia was much more than simply a very warm human being; she was a keeper of the flame of human possibility.

Virginia had tapped into the Basic Pool of Energy of the Cosmos. In the introduction, I mention the parallel between Virginia's thinking and that of other great minds who have devoted their lives to attempts to wring Truth out of this trying world. These "meditations" reflect the spiritual nature of her work. In following her instruction, one can feel that grounding energy of the "below" and that inspirational energy of the "above"; in her other exercises, one could experience the energy of the "between" — the connecting energy between specific human beings at a specific point in time and place.

CONGRUENCE – CONNECTING ENERGY

This connecting energy is present when communication is congruent; in simpler language: real. If I feel bad, I *say* I feel bad, my face and body posture reflect the words I say as well as my internal experience. The same is true if the emotion is joy, fear, or sadness. This concept appears so ordinary that it may easily be dismissed. Of course, we all know what "real" means just as we know what sunrise and butterflies are. Yet, how often do we allow ourselves to seriously consider the miracle of life as it flits around our turning globe? Being "real," or communicating congruently, is both that recognizable as well as that intrinsically miraculous — which is one reason it is so difficult to define. However, a great many of us are so cut off from our feelings/bodies that we think "congruence" is an idea, rather than a teardrop; a thought, rather than a shiver; a mental construct, rather than a smile. In fact, congruent communication is *all* of the above; it is the *matching* of emotion, thought, words, body, facial expression. Virginia provided experiences to explain her concepts, always filling her work with images, wanting to breathe life into the learning process as yet another part of the living process.

"Congruence" is no more, and no less, than being all of who we are at a given point in time with another human being. Congruent communication is a committed, active pursuit of clarity of meaning with another person. That pursuit presupposes and includes clarity of one's *self* with one's self. In*tra*personal congruence is as important as in*ter*personal congruence in the making of meaning between people.

Self esteem, communication, and system rules are all so interrelated that intervening in one makes a change in the other. Intrapersonal congruence has to do with the rules one learned in one's own family system; many families have "rules against" various feelings. In many families it is "not o.k." to be angry. In others it is permitted to be angry, but not to be afraid, and so on. Since there is no such thing as "stopping" a feeling, awareness of such an "unacceptable" feeling may bring shame, lowering self-esteem as a consequence. Thus, it is not the *feeling* that brings the lowering of the self-esteem; it is the *feeling* about the *feeling*.

A friend, who had spent a weekend at one of Virginia's seminars once asked me, "What is so great about being congruent? Why would anybody want to be congruent?" At that point, I realized that one was very unlikely, in one weekend exposure, to have learned those "teachable, learnable" skills of communication that Virginia did so ably teach. Participation in one of her longer seminars, such as the Avanta Process Communities, was necessary to learn those quite learnable skills. People, so often, are looking for technique in a weekend exposure to a master "craftsman." Virginia was not about technique; she was about essence. A particularly literal-minded person could very well miss the point. The very simplicity of what Virginia was offering could serve to obscure it.

Understanding the components of congruent communication and being able to recognize the presence of the four very specific, recognizable patterns of incongruent communication was, I believe, a major part of Virginia's "magic," not only as therapist, but as a human being in interaction with other human beings. Virginia's own caption for her work was: Becoming more fully human. Communication, purged of inhuman rules, serves that end.

The following is a description of Virginia's observations — those important discoveries — of the communication processes common to all people: the distinction that can and must be made between congruent communication and incongruent communication.

Congruent communication is a living, dynamic process than can no more be "caught" in time than can the growth of caterpillar to butterfly. As soon as one stops the action, one stops the life process. Discoveries in physics tell us that we cannot even *watch* a process without influencing the process, a "neutral observer" being a figment of imagination which can not exist in our world. Congruent communication, like Life itself, is dynamic, never static. Here is where Virginia's "psychological" work made interface with the spiritual. Congruent communication represents Life in motion, Life stepping from concept into living form; this was how and why Virginia would refer to a given human being as a "wonderful manifestation of Life."

Conversely, *in*congruent communication follows an old and *rigid* pattern, is an old script pulled out of a pocket left from childhood — an "old learning" about coping with the stress of threatened self-esteem.

All communication takes place within a given context. Nobody has the ability to step off the planet or outside the known universe and carry on a conversation. The congruent pattern of communication is always appropriate to what is going on *at the time*; within both "selves," between both "selves," and within the greater *context* within which the interaction is taking place.

This is why it follows, understanding that client and therapist are *both* members of the therapy system, that work on the self is no less important for the therapist than "work on" the client. This understanding transforms "work on" to "work *with*." With the broad understanding of general system theory (von Bertalanffy, 1971), a given client is understood to be not only a part of a system in which the therapist is another part, but that *both* are part of the greater context. This "part of" phenomenon extends not only to being "part of" a given family; not only part of the rest of the world, but of the *Cosmos*. With her broad vision, Virginia understood we are all part of the Larger Story. Therefore, she was always looking for the whole.

Virginia's unrelenting belief in the inherent value of each unique person had to do with her ability to see the bigger picture. That belief would lead the person with whom she worked toward the deeper truths in his/her family. Virginia's deep respect for Beingness as manifest in the specific person before her, served as a compass point to lead through that which manifests as "pathology" to reveal a disguised and ineffectual wish, on the part of all people, to communicate, to share the inner experience with the other once a safe context is created.

Being able to distinguish between the life-enhancing nature of congruent communication versus the life-endangering nature of incongruent communication is — literally, over the long haul — as worthwhile a piece of information as being able to distinguish one form of mushroom from another when gathering them in the woods (Brothers, 1987, 1988a, 1988b). It is the means for the creation of safety in context.

INCONGRUENCE — DISCONNECTING ENERGY

Incongruent communication (chart 1) is much easier to explain than is the far less prevalent, constructive form of interaction previously described.

Incongruent communication consists of placating, blaming, becoming super-reasonable, or becoming irrelevant in the face of selfworth questions.

Placating

It was Virginia's observation that about half the people she encountered would, when under emotional stress, sell themselves out to please the other person; the immediate response would be, "My own opinion — ideas, wants, needs — can not be as important as yours are." The range of possibility for this response of "I am not worth it [read: your time]," extends from sickeningly sweet, patronizing "agreement" to suicide.

Blaming

The next most popular response is to blame the other instead, trying to gain a sense of importance at the expense of the other. Although the outer message is, "*You* are not worth it and *I* am!"

CHART 1
Satir: Pictures of Interaction

My feelings
don't count.
(Placating)
Self is neglected,
crossed out.

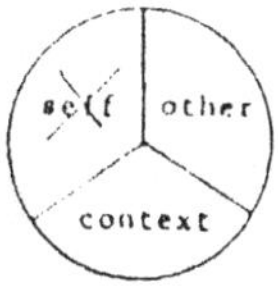

Your feelings
don't count.
(Blaming)
Other is neglected.

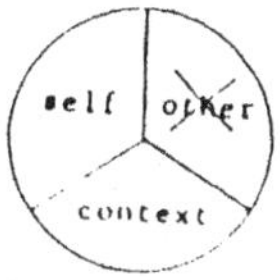

Feelings
don't count.
Only the context
or task counts.
(Super-reasonable)
Persons are neglected.

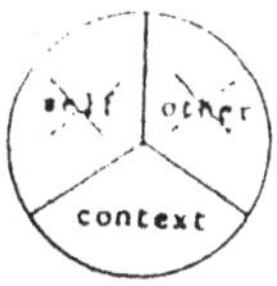

Nothing
counts.
(Irrelevant)
All reality
is neglected.

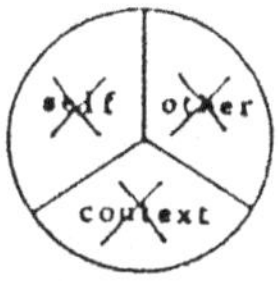

My feelings
count,
your feelings
count,
the context
counts.

the *inner* fear is, "How am I measuring up?" Although this stance bears the *seeds* of self-care, its alienating nature mitigates against connection with the other. Carry this behavior far enough and you go beyond disagreeableness and on to homicide.

Being Super-Reasonable

A response which is often more frequent among the intellectually gifted is to drain the dialogue of all feeling and focus on the "task" instead. In the feelingless response, the context becomes more important than the human beings involved. Many people in our culture equate this with an "adult" response and do not understand the serious danger presented to the physical aspect of the self in chronic use of this response to the self-worth questions. In Virginia's homespun words, "there is a gland for every feeling and a juice for every gland; dry up the feelings and you dry up those juices" (Personal communication, 1971). Do it over enough years and your body begins to suffer the literal consequences of the diminishment of those various juices. Thus this response is not only ultimately quite dangerous for the larger society — it permits the behavior of terrorists and all those who believe ends justify means — it is dangerous for the bearer in the physical consequences; may even end in cancer (Brothers, 1987, 1988a).

Being Irrelevant

A certain percentage of any population will, when feeling low in self-worth, begin to behave irrelevant to the subject and persons at hand as well as to their own feelings. This irrelevance is accomplished by distracting behavior and the hope is to avoid being noticed at all rather than to be noticed and found wanting. In the farthest extremes of this behavior lies florid psychosis.

PHYSICAL IMPLICATIONS

All of the incongruent responses or stances have physical consequences; our emotions are not separate from our bodies. There is a physiological response to every feeling we have (or do not have, given a long enough absence). Not only do our relationships, both familial and international, suffer when we are stuck in our static incongruent stances, our *physical* selves suffer. This is the way physical pain can be seen as communication and received as an important message.

> Communication is the giving and receiving of information between two people. That's how it always goes. It is just giving and receiving information. When someone coughs, what kind of information does the other one receive? Just ask yourself that. If you go beyond words and think about it, when you cross your legs, or you uncross your legs, or lift your head, or say 'poof,' or your skin color changes, or you get a lump some place, no matter what, all of that is a communication the giving and receiving of information . . .
>
> . . . I get that all over the world. I have [for example] been able to supervise Swedish speaking therapists with Swedish speaking families and pick up all the discrepancies, because the language is not all there is. What I get is that I see the body. In order to give dysfunctional body language, the body is "out of sync." I look at the jaw muscles, I look at the mouth . . . I hope you will learn how to observe without judging, but just to see. The minute that a self is congruent, everything about that body is relaxed. . . . [What makes all the difference is] the *awareness* of the split message, the double message . . . (Satir, 1987, tape 5)

CONGRUENCE – TRUTH

If the split message is not heeded and the gap between truth and psychological/physical posture corrected, the message may become more insistent in terms of physical distress. This is not some kind of metaphysical "punishment for not telling the truth." This is a physiological consequence of a particular stress on a particular organ and/or bodily part.

The understanding of this relationship of truth – congruence – to health/growth is an important part of the legacy Virginia left. These observations and explications of these, the five universal patterns of human communication are the method behind Virginia Satir's extraordinary ability to connect and to facilitate connection. This was the information she left behind: teachable, learnable skills about how human communication works.

Truth is such a *rare* thing it is delightful to tell it.

— Emily Dickinson

REFERENCES

Brothers, B.J. (1987). Independence *avoids* intimacy: Avoidance of intimacy kills. *VOICES: the Art and Science of Psychotherapy*, 23(1), 10-23.

Brothers, B.J. (1988a). The cancer patient is the self-contained patient. *Psychotherapy Patient*, 4(3/4), 227-241.

Brothers, B.J. (1988b). Remorse and regeneration. *Psychotherapy Patient*, 5 (1/2), 47-62.

Dickinson, E. (1958). Letter 342a. *The Letters of Emily Dickinson.* Vol.II, p.474, Cambridge: The Belknap Press of Harvard University Press.

Satir, V. (Speaker). (1987). Avanta Process Community VII, Module I. (Cassette recording #5). Crested Butte, Colo.: Blue Moon Cassettes.

Satir, V. (Speaker). (1982). (Unpublished transcript of cassette recording). Crested Butte, CO: Avanta Process Community II, Module I.

Satir, V. (1988). *The New Peoplemaking.* Mountain View, CA: Science and Behavior Books.

von Bertalanffy, L. (1971). *General Systems Theory.* London: Allen Lane.

Theory and Practice
of the Satir System

Yetta M. Bernhard

SUMMARY. A brief overview of the theory and practice of the Satir System showing the major dynamics of past and present family systems; how the present is influenced by past learnings—conscious and unconscious; the many innovative ways creating the possibilities of new views of old matters; the concept of taking responsibility for behavior changes in meeting the realities of the present more productively.

Virginia Satir considered herself a detective investigating the dynamics of family living. Her basic thesis was: One learns in the family particular behaviors and beliefs and methods of coping with each other. She maintained that information gets transmitted not only verbally but through all our senses. Dissonance arises when body messages (facial expressions, nervous gestures, etc.) belie the spoken words. Satir continually illustrates her basic thesis by demonstration—using her audiences as participants in relevant scripts that she spontaneously creates. Satir views the family as an essen-

---

Yetta M. Bernhard, PhD, received her education at Temple University, with graduate work at Columbia University, The University of Pennsylvania, Anglo-American Institute of Moscow University, Claremont Graduate School of Psychology, American Institute of Family Relations, the Institute of Group Psychotherapy and International College. She was a workshop leader and visiting instructor at many universities in the United States and Canada. She is Conflict Management Consultant to professional, educational, and business organizations. She is co-author with George Bach, PhD, of *Aggression Lab* and is the author of *How to be Somebody* and *Self Care*, published by Science and Behavior Books, 2017 Landings Drive, Mountain View, CA 94043. Correspondence may be sent to 5285 Village Green, Los Angeles, CA 90016.

tial topic of research. Each family, over generations, passes on mores, morals and attitudes that are absorbed consciously and unconsciously. To surface such unconscious learnings Satir choreographs "Family Reconstructions: These are psycho-dramas based on real and imagined family interactions and emotional conflicts which bring to light the milieu in which parents, grandparents, great grandparents, uncles, aunts, siblings operated in the various generations. Such evolved knowledge of one's family history de-mystifies the question of "Who am I." A basic focus of the Satir System is on careful research of family development generally and specific families particularly. She maintains that stress is increased as the family increases in number making it necessary for each family member to make room for the new member. She taught that to study each family it is necessary to probe for the hidden messages; the family secrets; (who knows what?); the alliances made to create support systems; the designated sick, crazy or family misfit; the impact of deceased members and absent members. Another item of investigation is the power structure in the family. The assumed dichotomy of dependency and autonomy often becomes a survival issue. Character is developed in the process of learning to survive and to cope with the realities of one's particular family. Out of this process one learns to placate, to blame, to compute, or to distract as primary methods of self preservation. In each of these primary methods of survival Satir asserts there are somatic correlates. The stress of maintaining a characteristic mode of behavior is felt physically and adds to or intensifies particular bodily weaknesses and illnesses.

Another focus of the Satir System is on intrapsychic conflicts and the internal wars they provoke. This is dramatically illustrated in one of her many innovative "games." Her Parts Party game is designed to dramatize the different pulls within human beings and the many possibilities of transforming destructive aspects of oneself into more productive ways of being and behaving. The Parts Party is one of many exercises innovated by Satir to help deepen self awareness and to experience alternative ways of looking at what is in order to fashion new realities. The idea of available options is emphasized. Satir maintains that we have the power to use what is destructive to transform such destructive behavior into more productive channels. Such transformation is accomplished in many ways: by a change in perception based on a new insight; by creation of a new vocabulary (the power of words to alienate or bond is stressed); to show the possibility of other options available.

Through various forms and modalities the Satir System probes the dynamics of families and family members. Specifically she innovates psychodramas: choreographs family connections through "Living Statues" showing who is close to who, who is isolated, who is dependent on whom, etc. She expertly combines knowing and doing, and insists the power for creative growth exists in every individual and family.

The Satir System emphasizes that the process of working out of dysfunction is the process of making choices and looking at alternatives. A family operating as a closed system shuts the door to other choices and alternatives and leaves no road out of stress. Change comes by way of death or outside intervention. The job of the therapist is primarily education for change.

Information about family pressures, Satir insists, is a major source in effecting change. Such information is elicited in many innovative ways. Virginia Satir often becomes the director of scenes she creates of simulated or real families in stress. These are designed to demonstrate the process of communicating feelings about specific pressures. In such a psychodrama family members are encouraged to talk to each other about what it means to be in their particular family under their particular circumstances. She makes clear that when feelings are not shared one doesn't know the other. Getting information opens the door to doing something about the information. New choices mean change. Change is growth in the process of attaining the power and freedom of standing on one's own feet. Such a family drama highlights the fact that what happens in a family under stress is experienced and assessed differently by family members. Mixed messages are often received. Communication clarification is a necessity as a process in effecting change. This is emphasized again and again — as is the importance to work constantly in process. The family is viewed as a constantly evolving process.

The purpose of all of Satir's methodologies is to determine people in stress:

- What did you see and feel?
- What happens when something new is added in a family relationship?
- What new communication emerged?

The problem of getting family members in touch with feelings, and of breaking down resistance to change is frequently met by therapists. The process of building trust and considering other choices through empathic listening is a developed art. Such empathic listening often discloses the possible meaning of resistance to change. This resistance might be an attempt at self protection. This, in turn, opens the possibility of probing for information. What is one protecting? Is it necessary? Are there other possibilities? Satir asserts that growth is a process of removing obstacles to realistic goals.

A Family System, Satir states, is a process made up of action, reaction and interaction. A closed system upholds the status quo, an open system is one that integrates change. "Open" means choice to be open or closed at times.

Satir teaches that mental health or mental illness is determined by how we look at what is human, how we look at issues, and how we cope.

The purpose of the Satir System of Therapy is to make understood and incorporate as process her five freedoms:

1. The freedom to see and hear what is there instead of what should be, was, or will be.
2. The freedom to say what one feels and thinks, instead of what one should.
3. The freedom to feel what one feels, instead of what one ought.
4. The freedom to ask for what one wants, instead of always waiting for permission.
5. The freedom to take risks in one's behalf, instead of choosing to be only 'secure' and not rocking the boat.

This becomes an ongoing procedure for life.

To implement the five freedoms, Virginia Satir emphasizes, that a new communication is necessary—a communication that clearly discloses how I feel about me, how I feel about you and me, how I feel about my physical being, and how I feel about my ability to cope. The ability to communicate freely starts with knowing oneself and becoming aware of another—an ongoing process of self and other knowing.

All Satir's emphasis is on teaching and learning how to cope with life's experiences more effectively and less destructively. She calls this a process of making people more human. Learning to cope more productively makes possible some realization of the message in one of her many posters:

> I want to love you without clutching
> Appreciate you without judging
> Join you without invading
> Invite you without demanding
> Leave you without guilt
> Criticize you without insulting
> If I can have the same from you then we can truly meet and enrich each other.

Total realization of such wants would mean attaining perfection. Satir makes clear that striving for perfection as a goal in life, is both too stressful and realistically unattainable. The process of coping and learning continuously to change what is found to be possible and to live around what cannot be changed is the road to becoming more human. This process set in motion by all families and heads of governments comprising a world family, offers the possibility of attaining world peace.

The Triadic Concept in the Work of Virginia Satir

Michele Baldwin

SUMMARY. For Virginia Satir the primary family triad is the major source of learning during the developmental years. In spite of the difficulties inherent in its structure, the triad holds the potential of being a great source of strength and nurture for the individuals involved. The various ways in which Virginia has used the triadic concept in her work are discussed.

In recent years, Virginia Satir has used the triadic concept as a cornerstone of the theoretical framework of her approach to therapy (Satir & Baldwin, 1983). She has not been alone in her view of the importance of the triad in our world. Its importance has been recognized in religion (Adam, Eve and the Serpent, the Holy Trinity), in the harmonies of Western Music (Len Holvik, personal communication, March 4, 1984), in physics, in psychology (Bowen 1978) and in sociology (Simmel 1902, 1950, Caplow 1969). However, whereas most authors have tended to perceive the triad with a feeling akin to the way Christians look at Original Sin, Virginia has viewed the triad in a more positive light.

In this paper, I propose to discuss the importance of the triadic concept in Virginia's work in the following manner: First, I will define the triad, indicating how it differs from the monad and the

Michele Baldwin, LCSW, PhD, is Assistant Professor of Psychiatry and Behavioral Sciences, Northwestern University Medical School and is on the Faculty of The Family Institute. She is also a psychotherapist in private practice. She had a long relationship with Virginia Satir with whom she co-authored *Satir Step by Step* and the *Use of Self in Therapy*. She is a trainer of the Satir-Avanta Network. Correspondence may be sent to 1550 N. Lake Shore Drive #18G, Chicago, IL 60610.

dyad. Second, I will show how the primary family triad is the major source of learning during the developmental years. Third, I will indicate how, in spite of its inherent difficulties, the triad holds the potential of being a great source of strength and nurture for the individuals involved. In fact, Virginia has felt strongly that therapy can be viewed as the art of healing the original triad. As the issues raised in the primary triad become understood in their original context, they serve to illuminate rather than contaminate the present. Finally in the last part of this article, I propose to discuss the various ways in which Virginia has used the triad to help people, be they patients, students, or anyone interested in developing their humanness, to learn and to use their triad for nurture and growth.

I. WHAT IS A TRIAD?

In many ways the triad can be seen as the foundation of all societal life. Many theorists describe family life as a set of interlocking triangles. Indeed, the operational complexity of even the smoothest functioning family is due to the number of interactions and perceptions which occur following the birth of the first child. Let us take a look at this complexity. Before an individual (monad) enters into a relationship with another, he[1] acts as his own unit of expression and decision. His thoughts, feelings and actions are based on his own perceptions ("How I think/feel about me"). When two individuals meet and form a couple, three units of perception and communication come into existence: two monads and one dyad, ("How I think/feel about you and me"). The minute the child is added, the interactions become vastly more complex: The three person system is comprised of seven structural units (three monads, three dyads, one triad) and many more operational units. In each of the three monads, father, mother, and child, the operational question is; How does mother, think/feel about herself, how does father think/feel about himself, and how does child feel/think about himself. In the three dyads, mother-father, mother-child, and father-child, the operational questions are: How does mother think/feel/act towards her husband, how does she think/feel/act towards her child? How does father/think/feel/act towards mother, towards his child? How does the child think/feel/act towards his mother, towards his father?

Let us now focus our attention on what happens in the triad: Operationally, we have the triad formed by the mother and father as they relate to the child, the triad formed by the mother and child as they relate to the father, and the triad formed by the father and child as they relate to the mother. The complexity of perceptions and questions that arise in a three person family increases further when one considers the number of perceptions held by each of those three people. Not only do father, mother and child have perceptions of themselves and of each other, they also have thoughts about how the two others perceive them, thoughts which have an impact on their behavior. As additional children are born, or if the child is part of an extended family, the complexity of triadic formation increases geometrically and so does the complexity of family interactions. The accompanying illustration shows how a family of more than three is made of sets of interlocking triangles (Bowen, 1978; and Caplow, 1969).

DAD   MOM

KID

KID

KID

II. THE LEARNINGS
IN THE PRIMARY TRIAD

In this section we propose to review the learnings which occur in the primary triad and to look at the process by which they happen.

The reason Virginia Satir puts so much emphasis on the primary triad of father, mother and child is that the triad is the place where the individual begins the formation of his personhood and his self-concept. On the basis of his experience in the primary triad, the child determines his place in the world and how much he can trust his relationships with other people.

It is essential to note that although it may appear superficially that a child only needs one parent (usually the mother who nurses him), the father (or memory of the father) plays an important role from the beginning. Indeed, the quality of the mother's care depends on what goes on (or went on) between her and the child's father. Also, if there are more children and/or if the child is part of an extended family, the same basic principle applies, but in a more complex form. The child is then a part of multiple triadic systems, although under those conditions one triad will usually be foremost.

When the child enters the world he is absolutely helpless and completely dependent upon the experiences, the directions and the behaviors of the two people (even if one is present only in memory or in imagination), who are there to steer his course. In this state of total dependency, his survival depends on the care he receives from his parents. Any adult, regardless of how deprived he was in his early childhood, had to receive some care as an infant: a minimum of food and love were needed for his physical and emotional survival.

As a result, the first vivid images he forms of his parents are that they are all powerful, as evidenced by their size and their ability to provide or withhold love and care. Regardless of the benevolence and love of the parents, all early experiences of the child occur in a context where he is weak and helpless. The most loving intentions of any parent cannot spare their child the realization that the human condition eventually has to be faced by each individual alone. He uses what he sees, hears and understands to form images of the world around him.

These powerful experiences, totally unconscious during the first months of life, become more and more conscious as the child grows. Since it is in the nature of humans to try to make sense of what happens to them, the child will make up whatever he does not understand. Later, the conscious and unconscious memories of childhood become an interesting blend of truth and distortion, which may affect his self and world view, as well as his ability to cope throughout his whole life. A child who experiences feelings of abandonment during his first months of life might have difficulties in forming close trusting relationships later on in life for fear (often unconscious) that he might be abandoned again. If he has given himself the explanation that those feelings of abandonment were the result of lack of love, he may give himself the message that he is not lovable.

It is also in the primary triad that early in life the child develops coping mechanisms to deal with stress. These learnings will determine how the individual copes with the world around him, unless they are replaced by new learnings. It is important to note, however, that unconscious, especially pre-verbal, learnings are the most difficult to undo.

To illustrate, let us give birth to an hypothetical child, Charlie. We will examine how his personhood, identity and self-worth develop as a result of growing up in a triad. We will also describe how he develops his feelings about himself and his learnings on how to relate to others in the primary triad. From the way his mother treats him, he will learn what to expect from women. In Eriksonian terms, during his first weeks of life, he will learn about basic trust or mistrust. He will also learn how to please and displease his mother, and this may well become the model of how to please or displease other women in his life.

From the way his father treats him, Charlie will learn what to expect from men. If he has a very domineering father (or if he perceives his father to be so, because of his large size, loud voice, etc . . .) he may grow up afraid of other men, or at least of men in the position of authority over him. While many other variables will be responsible for shaping the final outcome of Charlie's relationship to men later on, from observing his father, Charlie will also form his images about what it means to be a father. His future fathering of sons may well be determined by that model, whether he accepts it as such, or reacts against it. Indeed, this will be true, unless Charlie is able later on to bring to consciousness these early learnings and replace them by new ones. Only when that happens can our adult Charlie freely make choices on how to do the fathering of his own children.

The way Charlie's parents treat each other gives him the model of how men and women relate. If his father blames or bullies his mother, he will find it difficult to act otherwise towards his future wife. If his mother always placates his father, he may well end up choosing a wife who placates him. Many variables will affect this outcome because of the large number of observations that he will make of the parental pair.

The reason for which triadic learnings are so complex is that what the child learns to expect from each of his parents when he forms a dyadic relationship with either one of them, may be quite different when their triad is in operation. As an example, let us look at what happens when Charlie sucks his thumb. Mary, his mother, knowing what a source of comfort his thumb is for Charlie, enjoys his contentment. However, Fred, his father (perhaps remembering a similar situation in his childhood) is very concerned about what this thumb will do to his son's teeth, and pulls it out of his mouth right away. So Charlie, who is a bright child, learns early in life not to suck his thumb in front of his father — at least when he remembers. This may present him with some discomfort, (he may even try to avoid his father), but not necessarily with conflict, because he has already accepted the fact that his parents hold different expectations of him. A problem, however, arises for Charlie when he sucks his thumb in front of both his parents when they are together. Several scenarios are possible, and each of them will have different consequences for Charlie's development.

In the first scenario, Fred and Mary, who dearly love each other, and for whom love means that disagreements should be avoided, don't say anything, and Charlie learns that if he wants something from his father, he should always ask for it when his mother is present because his father won't say no.

In the second scenario, Fred holds Mary responsible for Charlie's thumb sucking. He thinks that she is an irresponsible or incompetent mother, or possibly that she deliberately allows Charlie to suck his thumb to spite him. So he tells Mary: "Get that thumb out of your son's mouth." If Mary does so, Charlie will learn that if he wants something from his mother, he is better off asking when his father is not around. Or, Mary may tell Fred "Why don't you do it yourself," and Charlie may watch his parents get into a fight which no longer has anything to do with his thumb, but with the question of who has the right to tell whom what to do. Charlie now learns that he can cause trouble between his parents — and feel guilty or powerful as a result. He also learns that when his parents get into a fight, he is no longer in the hot seat.

In a third scenario, Fred may object to the thumb, but when Mary replies: "I don't agree, I think it is comforting for Charlie to suck his thumb," Fred drops the conversation. In this case, Charlie will learn that his mother is likely to be his advocate and source of support, and decide to give his trust to her. The flip side of that coin is that Charlie may grow up to believe that women hold the real power in the family and that men are weak.

The episode of the thumb sucking is a microcosm of the many issues that come up in child rearing. It provides an illustration of the process by which Charlie learns about his own power, or lack of it, and how to behave in the world. In the above three scenarios, he learns about potential coalitions with one parent against the other. He also becomes aware of different forms of manipulation that he can use in many situations. Needless to say, if we had used a girl rather than a boy in our example, the process would have been the same with some possible differences in outcome. Such differences would be due to the fact that the modeling which occurs from the parent of the same sex has a different impact than the modeling which comes from the opposite sex parent.

Fortunately, the above scenarios are not the whole story. A more positive outcome is possible as we will examine in the next section in which we describe how the nurturing triad operates.

The foundation of Charlie's self-esteem, how Charlie feels about himself, is also acquired in his primary triad. Indeed, one of the characteristics of the triad mentioned earlier is that one person may feel excluded in certain situations. Although these feelings are also true for Mary and Fred, we will focus our attention here on Charlie, because our focus here is on his development into adulthood. Let us describe the mechanism by which this occurs. Most meaningful communications in the primary triad take place between two people at a specific moment in time: mother-father, mother-child, or father-child. If Charlie feels excluded from many interactions between Fred and Mary, he may perceive this exclusion as a rejection, think of himself as unlovable, and develop low self-esteem. He may feel that whenever he is not at the center of a triadic interaction, the two other members of the triad have something better going. Such feelings are stressful and may lead Charlie into using dysfunctional and incongruent responses. He may ignore or deny the feelings, he may blame his parents for not loving him, or distort the reality of his experience.

The primary triad, then, is the place where children first learn about inclusion and exclusion, which gives them a sense of their place in the world. Unless modified by subsequent learning experiences, these learnings will shape their personality.

III. THE NURTURING TRIAD

Charlie's experience has demonstrated that life in the primary triad is fraught with difficulties and can result in potential problems for adult life. We will examine later some of the corrective measures through which Charlie may acquire new learnings which may help him to function more effectively as an adult. Our purpose in this section is to show that, despite the potential problems that can arise in a dysfunctional primary triad, it is possible to raise children who will grow up as adults with high self-esteem. Learning how to develop a nurturing triad is the foundation of mental health, for individuals, families and society.

The primary triad can be a place where everyone can feel good about themselves and where the forces of cooperation are strong. In such a triad, all three people agree to put their resources together and create a basket of possibilities from which they can draw as needed. The structural ingredients in such a triad are not different from those of the dysfunctional triad. The difference lies in the process by which such a triad operates, which results in high self-worth for all its participants.

Let us review the characteristics of the healthy triad. We can look upon them as guidelines for good mental health and prevention. The first characteristic of the healthy triad is that of the freedom to comment and to respond. It is always possible for any individual within the triad to state his feelings without being put down. In a respectful atmosphere a child can let his parents know that he is feeling left out. This does not mean that his parents have to interrupt what they are doing to include him, but rather, that they can acknowledge his feeling state, and then be able to respond in the way which best fits the context of the situation. In such a triad, the words "yes" and "no" represent the reality of the moment and are not used as a symbol of love or lack of it.

The second characteristic of the healthy triad is that any one of the three persons is free to comment on his perceptions of a situation and/or check out their validity. The importance of this characteristic comes sharply into focus when one realizes that, in a dysfunctional triad, the inability to check out the validity of one's perceptions leads to treating such unchecked perceptions as if they were facts. The more dysfunctional the triad, the more likely communications will occur at the most complex level of perceptions seen as facts. A wife, for instance, whose husband forgets their anniversary, might conclude that he no longer loves her. If treated as a fact, this perception could snowball into severe communication problems, whereas a simple question might reveal her husband's intense preoccupation with a business problem about which he feels helpless.

The third characteristic of a healthy triad is that there is no rule of conformity. Each of its members is allowed to think, feel, behave and grow in his own way. In the example above, when Charlie sucks his thumb in front of both parents, Fred would share with Mary his concern that thumb sucking could lead to orthodontic problems. Mary might answer that her chief consideration is the comfort that Charlie receives from sucking his thumb. After sharing their different views on the subject, they might look at ways in which they could provide comfort differently, or find some method for limiting the thumb sucking. By watching this interaction, Charlie can learn a lesson in respectful handling of differences and know that, regardless of the outcome, he does not have to feel responsible for creating problems between his parents. He will also learn that it is possible for people to build understanding with one another instead of using their differences as weapons.

Finally, in the healthy triad, pairing can occur without major risks. The father feels happy to see what good care his wife takes of their child, and if he feels left out, he can comment upon it, rather than using this feeling to experience lowered self-worth. The mother can take pleasure in watching her husband and child enjoy an activity together and the child can know that his parents are entitled to share time together without his interference. In such a triad, the pairing is fluid in that it occurs within each of the three sets of triads. The person who is the "odd man out" at any moment knows that, given a little time, he too will be in the foreground. Undergirding these characteristics is an awareness of each individual as being the center of his own universe and a realization that this holds true for the other individuals as well. There is an acceptance of the basic dilemma of the triad: How to make room for three people, when only two can interact meaningfully at any one given moment. Human beings are not born with this knowledge: the infant only knows of his own needs. Parents have the important task to model for the child respect for the needs of others, as well as how to feel good about oneself when one is not the center of attention. As Virginia Satir states in *Peoplemaking* (1972):

> The challenge in family living is to find ways each individual can participate or be an observer of others without feeling he does not count . . . (p.152)

IV. THE PRIMARY TRIAD AS A TEACHER

After this discussion of the importance of the triad in the development of the individual, I would like to show how this concept is a major underpinning of Virginia's work.

In her training workshops,[2] the importance of the triad in the development of the individual's identity and self-worth is made very explicit. She has developed a series of basic exercises and many variations which illustrate the common feelings that arise out of being in a triad. The participants have an opportunity to get in touch with the way in which old pains and fears from their primary triad interfere with living their lives more fully, and can learn to communicate more congruently. The whole focus of the experience is towards the development of a nurturing triad. I will describe several such exercises, hoping to give the reader a flavor of how they work.

One exercise aims at making participants aware of the issues of inclusion and exclusion. People are asked to get into triads and to pay attention to how they feel when observing an interaction between the other two members of their triad. Sometimes they are told that they should form a primary triad of mother-father-child. Although such an exercise is very short in duration, the feelings evoked are often powerful. The observers often report to the other members of their triad that they felt left out, excluded, or even rejected. They may further state that although they wanted to be included, they were afraid to ask for fear that the answer might be "no." Sometimes, they may report that they started to withdraw from the situation. They may add that their reaction to the exercise parallels their reaction to similar situations in real life and that when this happens they often become resentful or envious of the relationship between the two others. Frequently, feelings from their early childhood get reactivated.

Many variations of this exercise can be developed. The observer may be put in a situation where he can mediate a conflict between the other two, thus gaining power. Or, he may be asked to find some way of attracting the attention of one or both other members to himself. Again the discussion following such an exercise is very relevant to real life.

Some triadic exercises clearly emphasize what can happen in a primary triad when father and mother disagree around the child. What happens to the child who is caught between two blaming parents, one a blamer and the other a placator, etc . . . ? Again, the feelings of every participant in the triad provide much insight into what happens to the child and/or each of his parents in a variety of universal situations.

The exercises mentioned so far usually do not reflect very positively on the triadic experience, because of the high probability of negative feelings in at least one, if not all the participants. There are other exercises which point out positive aspects of the triadic situation. This occurs when the individuals concerned possess a basic awareness of the human condition, in which they can accept being left out of a situation, and at the same time respect what ever feelings they may develop as a result of their triadic involvement. Once they can accept their feelings, they may be able to share them and the ability to comment is bound to bring about changes in climate.

In workshops of longer duration, the triad is both the major locus and focus of the training. Indeed, any therapist or person who wishes to use Virginia Satir's approach in their professional or personal life, needs to have fully explored the triadic processes in his primary, as well as more contemporary triads. He needs to fully understand how triadic processes affect human interactions and he needs to work out or, at least fully appreciate, how triadic forces shape his own life. Over time, most triads will surface some learnings that are destructive, painful or unfitting. They act as a stimulus which allows one to take a new look at things in oneself. The triad offers an excellent laboratory for helping its members to recognize, understand and become sensitive to old pains and fears, as well as to increase their ability to communicate more congruently.

In terms of procedure, participants usually are given the opportunity to select their triadic partners. Most triads, when they present themselves to the large group after a short time together, exude considerable euphoria at having begun to connect with two people towards whom they feel some positive attraction. After a short time, what usually emerges is that they were attracted by something familiar in the others. This "hat-hanging" phenomenon — transferring to a person in the present, the attributes of other people in one's past — is usually out of awareness and fairly innocuous in casual relationships. In more intensive relationships, such as one finds in intimate or work settings, as well as in the "triadic laboratory," familiarity eventually brings its share of problems. The familiarity is often based on a similarity — usually not consciously recognized — of characteristics belonging to a parent or a sibling. Thus, the chances are high that triadic partners will sooner or later find themselves in situations which elicit feelings which might "hook them," feelings which have nothing to do with the present triad.

Survival issues are those which arise for all of us when we are faced in the present by problems which we were unable to resolve in a distant past when we were helpless. When faced with survival issues, we often do not have access to the coping mechanisms which normally are at our disposal. Indeed, the chances are almost 100% that in an intense triadic relationship survival issues or stresses of early childhood will be reactivated. Sometimes the "hat-hanging" can be in the nature of a positive or negative stereotype or prejudice which, again, may have nothing to do with the present situation. A participant of the 1983 Summer Process Community described her experience as follows:

> With hindsight, I can see why I chose my triad . . . Jean appeared to me as the motherly type, stoic, intelligent and with a sense of humor. Dave's personality seemed similar to my father's — aloof, distant and intelligent . . . These two person-

alities together are familiar to me . . . The first indication of tension for me was in noticing how much of triad time was spent with Jean and Dave discussing their mutual activities together. I began to feel less than equal in the triadic relationship.

Through the process of the "triadic laboratory," participants have a rare opportunity to work through the problems they encountered earlier in life. As they begin to fully appreciate the nature of the triad, it becomes easier to accept that equal attention cannot be paid to each member at the same time. Most participants arrive with an understanding that, in many three person interactions, one person is left out, since only two people can be in direct physical contact with each other at any one moment in time. It is not, however, until the awareness and the existential pain connected with it becomes fully acknowledged, that the individual is able to transcend it and to engage realistically in the ebb and flow of human interactions.

In the exercises, triadic partners are guided to become aware of the feelings, thoughts and conclusions they draw when they are the one left out, such as, "do I feel unwanted?" or "if I withdraw, do I make negative judgments about the others or about myself?" or "do I have a positive attitude and enjoy my alone time?" or "do I remain involved and interested in what the two others are experiencing, waiting for the time I can be in direct contact with one or the other?" And, "if I choose to remain in direct contact, do I wait for an appropriate time, or do I inappropriately interrupt because I feel uncomfortable?"

Having recognized how each person reacts to the experience of being in a triad, participants are then encouraged to take advantage of the laboratory situation, which gives them permission to talk directly and clearly about what they are experiencing. In this process, it is possible for each person to develop an understanding of how the learnings of the triad of origin contribute to their intrapsychic development, as well as to their difficulties in relating to others. By becoming more aware of these past learnings and by being in a situation where, not only permission, but time is given to the task of sharing these feelings, the participants are often able to free themselves of these past learnings, and, instead of being ridden by compulsive behaviors, become aware of their choices. Another participant:

> The focus on the triad forced me to examine how I typically have used triadic situations to victimize myself and others. Looking at my primary triad, I can see that I learned to withdraw at the first sign of competition and to compete, not directly and honestly, but indirectly and duplicitously. I now see myself as an infantile Achilles sulking in his tent, or a child who wouldn't play a game because she could not be the leader.

Participants involved in this process sometimes need help to deal with the issues which may come up, especially at the beginning. Essentially, it consists of first helping each member of the triad to go through the process of becoming aware of an inner disquietude (the intensity might vary from very weak to very strong) in relation to the triad, and then to share this with the triadic partners. As perceptions and feelings get opened up in the triad, what often becomes apparent is that the discomfort stems from the pained member's inability to cope with a situation which he thinks would be simple to resolve, if it was not for the stubbornness (or other resistive quality) of one, or both of the other triadic members. The power struggle over trivial decisions can be a major problem. The need is for this person to think of past situations, when a similar feeling was present. This often takes the person back to his primary triad. By working with these feelings in relation to the past, a breakthrough in understanding the specific situation in the present triad often emerges.

In a month-long training situation, many ups and downs occur in the triads as participants move through deeper levels of awareness and transformation. The experience becomes even more powerful when triads are assigned specific tasks. Indeed, if they spend all their time processing feelings, the triadic participants end up operating in a vacuum which has little to do with real life situations. Many triads never experience actual conflict until they have to work together on a project. The process is often very trying, but in working it through, most participants develop deep attachment to their triadic learning companions. More important, they learn how to use invaluable tools which are available to them when they return to their home situations. The learnings which occur in the laboratory can be transferred to other triadic situations in real life and help these individuals to develop more nurturing triads.

Here is how a participant in one of the summer training programs described her experience:

> What I learned was an invaluable lesson in staying out of the middle and having confidence in each individual's ability to express his own feelings directly. When I arrived home after the Process Community experience, I had an opportunity to practice this new learning. The peacemaker role had always been a problem at work with my co-workers. I was able to verbalize my feelings and to take responsibility for staying out of the middle in disputes. I can now facilitate and use my skills in much more effective ways, making sure the people who have the issue are talking directly to each other and not through me.

Another of Virginia's interventions which is heavily based on the triadic concept is that of Family Reconstruction (Satir & Baldwin, 1983; Nerin, 1986). The major goal of a Family Reconstruction is to help a person understand and work through his early learnings, so that he no longer uses them compulsively in life situations which reawaken those past patterns. In the process of a Family Reconstruction, the person experiences not only the learnings of his original triad through a role playing process, but has an opportunity to witness the primary triadic learnings of each of his parents as well, since the process goes back into previous generations. The learnings of the primary triad then serve to illuminate the present rather than to contaminate it.

Virginia Satir's approach to Family Therapy relies heavily on working with the triadic formations within the family. There are many levels of triadic interventions in working with a family. They range from working with the existing triads present in the nuclear family to working with the primary triads of each of the parents. The goal of family therapy is to develop smoothly operating triads, with all of the healthy characteristics described earlier: triads in which it is possible for each one to comment freely, where the word "no" does not mean rejection, where communications are clear, and where each individual is allowed to be himself. In couples or individual therapy, this same triadic approach is also valid, in that the areas of life in which individuals experience coping difficulties usually go back to their primary triad.

In summary, the first part of this article attempted to demonstrate the importance of the triadic concept in Virginia Satir's approach to therapy and change. The second part was a description of ways in which this concept can be applied in many interventions.

NOTES

1. For ease of reading, "he" and "his" are being used in their neutral form, referring to "he" and "she" and to "his" and "hers."
2. In addition to her many workshops all over the world, since 1981, Virginia, and since her death, the Avanta Network, have conducted experiential month long training seminars in Crested Butte, Colorado.

REFERENCES

Bowen, M. (1978). *Family therapy in clinical practice*. New York: Jason Aronson.
Caplow, T. (1969). *Two against one: Coalitions in triads*. Englewood Cliffs, NJ: Prentice-Hall, Inc.
Nerin, W.F. (1986). *Family reconstruction long day's journey into light*. New York: W. Norton & Company.
Satir V. (1972). *Peoplemaking*. Palo Alto, CA: Science and Behavior Books.
Satir, V., & Baldwin, M. (1983). *Satir Step-by-Step*. Palo Alto, CA: Science and Behavior Books.
Simmel, G. (1902). The number of members determining the sociological form of the group. *American Journal of Sociology*, 8(1), 45-46.
Simmel, G. (1950). *The sociology of Georg Simmel*, by K.H. Wolff, Trans., Ed., and Introduction. New York: Glencoe Press.

While not specifically referred to, many of the ideas in this article have come from discussions with or presentations of Virginia Satir.

Virginia Satir's Triad Theory for Couples Therapy

Judith Bula Jacobs

SUMMARY. Virginia Satir's understanding of the fundamental building block of all human relationships, the triad, surpassed that of her colleagues. She went beyond their themes of conflict, opposition and pathology to emphasize the positive, constructive and nurturing potential of every human triadic interaction. Couples therapy is a triad and the author focuses on this specific context to illustrate some of the rich and varied uses of Satir's theory of triads.

INTRODUCTION

Virginia Satir (1916-1988) has left a vast legacy of knowledge, wisdom, skill, and her example of the goal of all of her work — being more fully human. From her self-stated beginnings at age five to be a "child's detective on parents" to the accumulated wisdom over her seventy-two years when the "detective work" had led to major efforts in bringing world peace alive, participants in her work and her life realize there is no aspect of human behavior which has not been touched by Virginia in some way. From the importance of self-esteem for the individual to congruent communication in interpersonal relationships to the empowering of agency personnel to her influence of national and international leaders, Virginia has been there. She not only spoke about and taught the multiple levels of all systems but she lived and acted at all those levels as well. No matter

Judith Bula Jacobs, PhD, is Assistant Professor, University of Denver Graduate School of Social Work, Denver, CO 80208. Correspondence may be sent to Dr. Judith Bula Jacobs, University of Denver Graduate School of Social Work, Denver, CO 80208.

43

at what point one chooses to focus, it is essential to bear in mind this holistic, universal perspective with which Virginia viewed her world. It was not unusual to hear her commenting on the similarities between two children fighting and then reconciling on the playground and two nations making declarations of war and peace. Her eye for similarities, however, did not blind her to the uniqueness inherent in each situation. In this uniqueness she was a true artist at discovering the potential and inevitable opportunities for growth, empowerment and purposeful change.

For this article, the chosen focus is on one of the most fundamental building blocks of Virginia's theory (as well as family therapy theory)—the triad. Readers are encouraged to allow their thinking to travel to all levels and contexts of application, as Virginia would have done, even though specific attention will be given to triad theory for the context of couples therapy here. The discussion begins with a review of various perspectives on triad theory from the beginning of family therapy theory. Then the specific concepts of Satir Triad Theory will be presented followed by their application to couples therapy. Though Virginia taught the universality of application of her triad dynamics to all triad situations, she did not specifically apply those dynamics for couples therapy (one couple, one therapist) in her writing nor have the contributions in her triad theory been applied to couples therapy by other authors in more than a passing manner. Offering such an application is the intended purpose of this article. Concluding remarks on future research will complete this presentation.

TRIAD THEORY IN FAMILY THERAPY

The intricacies, dynamics and effects of human transactional triads have been observed and studied from many different approaches. Social psychologist Heider (1958); sociologists Caplow (1968) and O'Connor (1974); family therapists Bowen (1957), Haley (1962), Satir (1964), Zuk (1966, 1971), Minuchin (1974); and couples therapists Sager (1976), Framo (1981), and Broderick (1983) all agree that the dynamics in a relationship among three people differ from those in a dyad or in a group of four and more.

Beyond this uniqueness as a unit, however, the triad receives some particular interpretations. The following discussion highlights some of these as given to us by several therapists who have identified the triangle as the "basic building block of any emotional (interpersonal) system" (Madanes and Haley, 1977, as quoted by Stanton, 1981, p. 365).

Murray Bowen presented the concept of "triangles" in 1957. At that time he used the term "interdependent triad." Later (1966) he went on to state that an "emotional system" such as a family is composed of a "series of interlocking triangles" (as quoted by Stanton, 1981, p. 365). From Bowen we learn that a triad forms when one member of a twosome internalizes the relationship tension and then seeks to "resolve" that tension by moving toward or more strongly investing in a relationship with a third person or thing, such as work or alcohol. He observed triads as characteristically having "two insiders and one outsider." Driving the process of the triad is the "emotional reactiveness of people and the level of emotion that gets attached to a particular issue" (Kerr, 1981, p. 242).

Haley, similarly, emphasizes the formation of a triad as happening "when tension between members of a two-person system becomes high, a third person is brought into the picture" (as quoted by Stanton, 1981, p. 365).

> Both Haley (1971, 1973) and Zuk (1966, 1971) have stressed the importance of the triangle or triad for conceptualizing 'psychological' problems and their treatment. Specifically, Haley notes that most child problems include a triangle consisting of an overinvolved parent-child dyad (a cross-generational coalition) and a peripheral parent. (Stanton, 1981, p. 365)

Salvador Minuchin's (1974) major contribution to the understanding of triads within family systems grows out of his concept of alignment, "joining or opposition of one member of a system to another in carrying out an operation" (Aponte, 1976, p. 434). Minuchin describes a particular kind of alignment called "triangulation." Once again we see the dysfunctional aspect of the triad emphasized in this description of Minuchin's use of triangulation by Aponte and Van Dusen (1981):

> In triangulation, each of two opposing parties seeks to join with the same person against the other, with the third party finding it necessary, for whatever reasons, to cooperate now with one and now with another of these opposing parties. Some of these dysfunctional structures involve more than one category of structural dimension as a dominant characteristic . . . (p. 314)

The theorists cited so far view the dynamics and processes of triads associated with tension, dysfunction, the conceptualizing of problems, and opposition. The last two theorists (Broderick and Satir) acknowledge the dysfunctional potential of triadic relationships but they also emphasize the strengthening and nurturing aspects of triads. Another difference between these two groupings of theorists is their view of the role of the therapist in the therapeutic triangle with the couple. For Bowen, Haley, Zuk and Minuchin the therapist acts in roles such as guide, director, educator, trainer or joiner. The triads recognized are outside the therapeutic triad—i.e., in the family-of-origin, with partner and/or children, in the workplace. Broderick and Satir recognize that the triad includes the therapist as one member of the therapeutic triad in couples therapy.

Broderick in his book *The Therapeutic Triangle: A Sourcebook on Marital Therapy* (1983) sometimes calls his format for working "triangular therapy." There are six components needing consideration when assessing the therapeutic triangle in the initial stages: (1) the wife (or partner A); (2) the husband (or partner B); (3) the therapist; (4) the marriage (or partnership); (5) the therapist's relationship with the wife (or partner A); and (6) the therapist's relationship with the husband (or partner B). "Each of the six, if ignored or mismanaged, can derail the therapeutic process" (p. 13). Broderick goes on to discuss the symmetrical relationship with the couple where "each client must feel EQUALLY accepted and supported" (p. 24). He acknowledges that the therapist cannot assume the capacity to intervene successfully until this "symmetrical rapport" is established. Regarding the role of the therapist, Broderick indicates "therapist potency — the power to turn the therapeutic process into a constructive course" (p. 38) — as a key factor in helping any couple move toward their goals. It is the role of a "coach" with "team members" which he finds most helpful.

Virginia Satir also recognizes the impact of triadic patterns across the life span and in multiple situations. The following discussions consider the various concepts of her triad theory and how they come alive in couples therapy.

VIRGINIA SATIR'S TRIAD THEORY

For Virginia Satir, triads just ARE. She has defined the triad as a "three-person learning system" (1983, p. 61). From the moment of conception, each human being is a part of multiple triads which are simply given in our complex transactional lives. She did observe that these triads may be used to function in unhelpful and problematic ways for the individuals in them but, additionally, she presents the qualities of a nurturing and supportive triad and the important ways therapists can enhance the process of transforming dysfunctional ways of being in triads into functional and satisfying ways.

An underlying belief of Virginia's approach to the world and the people in it is that "at any moment, an individual's thoughts, feelings, and behaviors are determined by longitudinal influences: the sum of his learning experiences since birth," and she views "the experience of the primary triad (father, mother, and child) as the essential source of identity of the 'self'" (Satir and Baldwin, 1983, pp. 169-170). From this essential source come the foundations for adulthood and the seeds for coping.

> On the basis of the learning experience in the primary triad, the child determines how s/he fits into the world and how much trust can be put in relationships with other people. For instance, a child who in the first months of life experienced many feelings of abandonment is likely to have a difficult time forming close, intimate relationships with others unless new learnings can replace the early experiences. It is also in the primary triad that early in life the child develops coping mech-

anisms to deal with stress. Most stress patterns that individuals experience in their adult lives have their origin in the cradle. (Satir and Baldwin, 1983, p. 170) (Paraphrased for inclusive language)

Also, it is in the primary triad where we first learn feelings of inclusion and exclusion. All members of the triad can have fears of being left out. " . . . there is no such thing as a relationship between three people. There are only shifting two-person relationships with the third member in the role of observer" (Satir, 1983, p. 73). Closely related to the inclusion-exclusion learnings are those about greater and lesser power and about loving and rejecting. Crucial to shaping thoughts and feelings about being in a triad is the meaning placed on being included or excluded. Distortions in learnings come when and if inclusion, for example, is taught to mean greater power and being loved and exclusion to mean lesser power and being rejected. Such equations are part of a recipe for low self-esteem or, at best, a self-esteem which is dependent upon circumstances rather than the person's own integrity. It is not physically possible for anyone to go through life being included, powerful and loved in every triadic situation experienced. "We are not like fish. We do not have eyes that look in two directions at the same time. Therefore, in the triad we can look first at one person and then at the other but we are not able to include both in our line of vision at the same time. This is a fundamental rule in all triads and in all relationships" (Satir, 1980).

In nurturing triads, however, the meaning placed on two members together and one in an outside or observing role carries explanations which take into account the context within which the triadic transaction occurs as well as the respective positions and roles of the members. Thus, mother can look on with approval or do other things while father and daughter (or son) have times together. Father can do the same. The children can be helped to see that mother and father need their time together as well without it being defined as a rejection of the child. In Virginia's classic example: "People who think they must always be included in what's going on with those other two over there don't understand one thing. You can't go to the bathroom that way" (Satir, 1980).

The nurturing triad remains nurturing by validating all of its units and relationships: each person as an individual; each dyad — mother-father (A-B); mother-child (A-C); father-child (B-C); and the three of them as a whole. This holds true for sibling triads, multi-generational triads; work-related triads, friendship triads and all other manner of relational triads, including the triad in couples therapy with one therapist and two members of the couple.

Inherent in maintaining this nurturing quality in relationships is Virginia's belief in the equality of value in each person. Personal value is not to be confused with differences in roles or positions. Referring to couples (pairs) she makes this point in the following way:

> . . . the ingredients of all successful and satisfying pairing are the same, whether the two people are lovers, parents, children, siblings, friends, or co-workers. These roles merely decide the form and context in which interaction takes place. Likewise, factors such as age, race, nationality, gender, and status serve simply to individualize each person. When pairing occurs between people who occupy unequal power positions, it is important to remember that their positions are not the same as their personal value. Personal value remains the same. (Satir, 1988, p. 332)

Differences in roles or positions often do get confused with personal value, though, and this is not uncommon among couples who request therapy. What we may hear them describe are the "power struggles" which have become part of their difficulty together. Moving from these places to the nurturing place described by Virginia's work will be discussed further in the following section on applications to couples therapy.

There is one other form of triad awareness given in Virginia's work which is an essential part of her triad theory and is helpful when considering couple dynamics: the three parts of every couple.

> Every couple has three parts: YOU, ME, and US; two people, three parts, each significant, each having a life of its own. Each makes the other more possible. Thus, I make you more possible, you make me more possible, I make us more possi-

ble, you make us more possible, and we together make each
other more possible. I find that love can truly flourish only
where there is room for all three parts, and no one part domi-
nates. (Satir, 1988, p. 145)

From this view of the you-me-us transaction, we see another of
Virginia's uses of systems thinking, specifically the reciprocal impact of all three parts on each other. Here also we see the importance of arriving at some sense of balance — no one part dominating.

These concepts reveal Virginia's attention to the healthy, functional, and nurturing side of triads. To summarize this section, it is
helpful to review her definitions of the "functional family triangle"
and the "dysfunctional family triangle" as well as the ingredients
of a nurturing triad.

- In the functional family triangle, the mates are confident about
  their own marital relationship and so are able, in an un-
  threatened way, to handle the child's fears of being left out.
- In the dysfunctional family triangle, the mates are not confident about their own marital relationship.
- I should add that although a son may appear closer to and
  allied with his mother (as a daughter may appear closer to and
  allied with her father) such an alliance is illusory.
- Because both mates in a dysfunctional family are particularly
  sensitive about being left out, the child does, in effect, end up
  by losing one parent unless he is able to reassure both parents
  by walking the precarious tightrope between them. (Satir,
  1983, p. 73)

For nurturing triads, Virginia observes the following characteristics:

- members know effective ways of handling their differences;
- each member values and feels valued by the other members;
- cooperation, not competition, is the nature of the interactions
  between members of the triad;
- each takes responsibility for her or his own actions;
- each member can be counted on to be emotionally honest;

- each member is able to communicate congruently (words and affect match); and
- each can comment on what is going on between and among them.

Longitudinal influences, meanings placed on inclusion and exclusion, equality of personal value, the you-me-us balancing, awareness of dysfunctional and functional behaviors and the ingredients of a nurturing triad offer important perspectives and tools for couples therapy. These are discussed further in the next section.

VIRGINIA SATIR'S TRIAD THEORY FOR COUPLES THERAPY

Couples therapy is a triad. When one therapist works with one couple, the experiential stage is set for all the possible dynamics of triad interaction to emerge. Awareness of such dynamics can mean the active participation of each triad member creating an effective, nurturing therapeutic triad rather than only observing pathological and dysfunctional uses of triads.

> Most individuals and families who come into therapy do not function effectively in triadic relationships. One of the purposes of therapy is to restore the individual's ability to function effectively in a triadic setting. (Satir and Baldwin, 1983, p. 174)

With this purpose in mind, the following discussion offers ways to bring this therapeutic goal alive with couples by shaping interventions grounded in longitudinal influence, helpful meanings of inclusion and exclusion, equality of personal value, balancing you-me-us, and promoting the ingredients of a nurturing triad.

Longitudinal influences are brought to the context of couples therapy by the therapist as well as by each member of the couple. Most family therapists and couples therapists in training are required to give attention to their own family-of-origin issues in order to separate them from the issues clients bring. It is essential to include a careful analysis of triads-of-origin, which include all significant emotional triads in the family-of-origin, in this aspect of therapist learning. Jane (not her real name) a 32 year old therapist working with Bob (age 42) and Mary (age 39) was confused by the apparent stuckness at the "social conversation" level with Mary and the "quiet, respectful distance" of Bob. When Jane was asked if there were other triads in her life of this nature, her immediate connection went to that of her sibling triad-of-origin. Her older brother and sister were the same ages as Mary and Bob and she acknowledged the wish to avoid deeper issues with both of her siblings. Jane removed these "hats" from Mary and Bob and found the work moving toward therapeutic goals once again.

Likewise, the clients come with influences from earlier triads in their lives and with the likelihood that functioning in those triads was not very effective. The possibility of repeating ineffective ways of functioning in the couples therapy triad is very high. Bob, the same Bob as above, came to therapy carrying the powerful influence of a "dominating mother and submissive father" while Mary described her parental triad-of-origin as "a strong connection with mom but dad was never around." Here, from all three members of the therapeutic triad, we see triad-of-origin themes which, if allowed to take their natural repetitive course, would lead to an alliance between the two women and Bob being distant, "absent," and/or submissive. And, in fact, this is what had happened until Jane, the therapist, introduced the parallels between the triad they were all in together for therapy and the triads-of-origin they each had brought with them from earlier experience. In separating what was past and what was present, they gained clarity in coping with the variety of issues at hand.

Similarities to transference and countertransference come to mind and certainly would not contradict Virginia's concept of longitudinal influence. Readers are referred to the work of Sager (1967) and Framo (1981) on the role of transference in work with couples. It is not timely to extend that discussion here but it is important to remind readers that the three-way triadic dynamic described here does present a different level of systemic complexity than the two-way transference-countertransference dynamic.

The *meaning placed on inclusion and exclusion* begins from the moment one member of the triad makes the initial contact with the therapist. It would come as no surprise that Mary was the one to make the initial contact with Jane and not Bob. By her doing so, both Mary and Bob were following their respective same-gender role models from their triads-of-origin: Mary by creating a strong alliance with "mother" (female therapist) and Bob by filling a "submissive" male role. Jane, as well, recognized a pattern of her sibling triad-of-origin as it was her sister who often called Jane requesting help in how to deal with their brother.

In the initial session Jane consciously worked to strengthen her bond with Bob and she communicated to both partners that they were equally included in the process. However, what every couples therapist soon realizes is that there is no way to anticipate the many meanings each partner brings from earlier triadic experiences of being included and excluded. Some examples are interpreting inclusion by being the same gender, same age, same ethnic or religious background, and same occupational status. When these characteristics differ, exclusion may be the interpretation. In an attempt to repeat her historic strong alliance with a female, Mary moved quickly to define her inclusion with Jane while excluding Bob. In the first two minutes of the session Mary had commented that she and Jane had attended the same college and she moved her chair to be closer to the therapist's and farther from Bob's. Bob did not make an effort to correct the imbalance, remaining consistent with his triad-of-origin dynamic.

The constant pull of defining by dichotomy rather than wholeness is clearly revealed in the dynamics of inclusion and exclusion. It seems to be especially powerful in work with couples probably because the couples often present their relationship as a living example of these dichotomies. It is the either-or, good-bad, dominant-submissive, close-distant way of perceiving which lies at the root of dysfunction in many relationships. Virginia's triad theory helps us to see that in the work with couples, therapist efforts of balancing the opposites are only one step. This step alone cannot be effective. The couple can always find other issues to continue to play out the "black-white" process. It is not until the process itself (that of needing to assume opposite stances) is addressed, plus a valuing of both extremes and all the shades of "gray" in between, that a therapeutic environment can exist. Therefore, an explanation, early in the contact with the couple, emphasizing the nature of our human condition to be able to engage with only one other person at a time plus the value of observations and feedback from the third person will help establish the triad as a nurturing and therapeutic one. For example, Jane, Mary, and Bob can each expect to be in that observing role at different times. That which, in dysfunctional triads, may be labelled as "exclusion" or "being left out" is seen in a functional triad as purposeful and necessary for the health of the triad. In the therapeutic triad in couples work, each member has permission to be in the observer role at any time with the therapist usually assuming that role more frequently as the couple's alliance with each other is strengthened.

Closely related is *equality of personal value*. Applying this to the context of couples therapy requires from the therapist an honest evaluation of where one's own personal value is in relation to that of the clients and, secondly, an active effort of helping to separate triad members' positions and roles from personal value.

Promoting equality of personal value between the members of the couple comes in the most congruent fashion from a therapist who holds that belief in the first place but who also models it in the therapeutic triad. This calls for the belief that the personal value of the therapist is neither greater nor less than that of the clients. Training of therapists which promotes an hierarchical relationship between therapist and clients can make the mistake of not being clear about the distinction between position and personal value. Positions differ and come with their related roles and tasks. Personal value remains the same. It is not uncommon to see beginning therapists placing themselves in a diminished role as they compare themselves with their client — "I am too young, I am too naive, I am too whatever." Whether the therapist elevates or diminishes herself or himself, the result is the same: personal value is not seen as equal.

Second, just as the therapist needs to clearly separate position from personal value for herself/himself, so does there need to be a watchful eye toward enabling the two partners in the couple to do the same. It is not unusual in initial sessions to hear the many ways the two partners are devaluing each other and often how they may be devaluing themselves as well. Much of the time one sees a confusion between position and personal value. Bob was without a job when he and Mary began therapy with Jane. It soon became apparent that this "position" had been expanded by both Mary and Bob to mean that Bob was a worthless person. Reminders of his other worthwhile contributions at home and in the community began to call into question the connection between unemployment and worthlessness.

Mary and Bob were similar to many couples who seem better able to articulate the "YOU" and "ME" of their relationship than they could the "US." Virginia has noted a balance among these three parts in functional relationships and an imbalance in dysfunctional ones. Mary and Bob discovered they had lost touch with their "US" when their two children were young. They reported that it had been approximately ten years since they had taken a vacation without their children or other relatives and nearly eight years for Mary and six years for Bob since they had felt satisfied with their sexual relationship. Their brainstorming about ways to achieve a greater balance came much easier than putting some of their creative ideas into action. It was in this effort that they began to discover that they are "meeting each other again after a long time."

Finally, within a nurturing context of purposeful inclusion and exclusion, separating position and personal value and balancing the "you-me-us" threesome, the therapeutic triad itself became a model for transforming other triadic relationships in Mary's and Bob's lives. Bob connected the loss of his job with an unresolved low self-worth feeling he had in his triad-of-origin with both his parents which had carried over into subsequent job interviews. First he confronted his own low self-worth/ personal value issue in the triad with Jane and Mary, then he did the same with his parents. His approach to the job interviews changed after that and within a month he had two solid offers to consider.

Mary reported a noticeable change in the way she related with their "quiet, shy" son. She began appreciating his quiet side instead of placing expectations on him to be otherwise.

Jane began the termination process with Mary and Bob when she recognized the qualities of the nurturing triad existing in their therapeutic triad. Differences were handled effectively, mutual valuing of each person was present, cooperation and congruent communication characterized the work, and there was freedom to comment about any subject.

As with any therapeutic work involving changes of long held patterns, these changes were not necessarily easy ones for Mary and Bob. Their experience is one, though, which illustrates the use of parallel information from triads-of-origin and present triads for clients and therapist alike.

To conclude, the words of the introduction are recalled: to allow our thinking to travel to all levels and contexts of possible application of Virginia's triad theory. For future research, these might include work with cross-racial, cross-ethnic, and homosexual couples; promoting the nurturing qualities in academic and work settings; and following Virginia's lead in observing the universality of triad dynamics at community, national and global levels. Transforming the destructive potential of the triad into constructive action may be one of the most important contributions we can make in these rapidly changing times.

REFERENCES

Aponte, H. (1976). Underorganization in the poor family. In P. Guerin (Ed.), *Family therapy: Theory and practice*. New York: Gardner.

Aponte, H. and Van Dusen, J. (1981). Structural family therapy. In A. Gurman and D. Kniskern (Eds.), *Handbook of family therapy*. New York: Brunner/Mazel.

Bowen, M. (1966). The use of family theory in clinical practice. *Comprehensive Psychiatry 7*, 345-374.

Bowen, M., Dysinger, R., Brodey, W. & Basmania, B. (1957). Study and treatment of five hospitalized families each with a psychotic member. Paper presented at the American Orthopsychiatric Association. Chicago.

Broderick, C. (1983). *The therapeutic triangle: A sourcebook on marital therapy*. Beverly Hills: Sage.

Caplow, T. (1968). *Two against one: Coalition in triads*. Englewood Cliffs, NJ: Prentice-Hall.

Framo, J. (1981). The integration of marital therapy with sessions with family of origin. In A. Gurman and D. Kniskern (Eds.), *Handbook of family therapy*. New York: Brunner/Mazel.

Haley, J. (1962). Family experiments: A new type of experimentation. *Family Process 1*, 265-293.

Haley, J. (1971). Family therapy: A radical change. In J. Haley (Ed.), *Changing families* New York: Grune and Stratton.

Haley, J. (1973). *Uncommon therapy: The psychiatric techniques of Milton H. Erickson, M.D., A casebook of an innovative psychiatrist's work in short-term therapy*. New York: W. W. Norton.

Heider, F. (1958). *The psychology of interpersonal relations*. New York: John Wiley & Sons.

Kerr, M. (1981). Family systems theory and therapy. In A. Gurman and D. Kniskern (Eds.), *Handbook of family therapy*. New York: Brunner/Mazel.

Madanes, C. and Haley, J. (1977). Dimensions of family therapy. *Journal of Nervous and Mental Disease 165*, pp. 88-98.

Minuchin, S. (1974). *Families and family therapy*. Cambridge: Harvard Press.

O'Connor, P. (1974). *Coalition formation in conjoint marriage counseling*. Unpublished doctoral dissertation, University of Southern California, Department of Sociology.

Sager, C. (1967). Transference in conjoint treatment of married couples. *Archives of General Psychiatry 16*, 185-193.

Sager, C. (1976). *Marriage contracts and couple therapy*. New York: Brunner/ Mazel.

Satir, V. (1980). Workshop presentation. Boston.

Satir, V. (1964). (1983). *Conjoint family therapy*. Palo Alto, CA: Science and Behavior Books.

Satir, V. (1988). *The new peoplemaking*. Mountain View, CA: Science and Behavior Books.

Satir, V. and Baldwin, M. (1983). *Satir step by step: A guide to creating change in families*. Palo Alto, CA: Science and Behavior Books.

Stanton, M. (1981). Strategic approaches to family therapy. In A. Gurman and D. Kniskern (Eds.), *Handbook of family therapy*. New York: Brunner/Mazel.

Zuk, G. (1966). The go-between process in family therapy. *Family Process 5*, 162-178.

Zuk, G. (1971). *Family therapy: A triadic-based approach*. New York: Behavioral Publications.

Enhancing the Marital Relationship: Virginia Satir's Parts Party

Joan E. Winter
Leanne R. E. Parker

SUMMARY. Satir viewed individuals, couples and families as isomorphic yet interrelated systems. The ability to focus on one component while impacting other systems remains a legacy of her work. Seeking to enhance an individual's autonomy and self worth, as well as enriching the marital relationship, Satir designed the Couples Parts Party. By attempting to surface the valued, alienated, extruded and unknown aspects of each partner, and assisting them in reclaiming and utilizing their diverse parts, this therapeutic intervention provides a potent catalyst for change. The Parts Party offers practitioners a diversified approach for enhancing the marital relationship.

A hallmark of Virginia Satir's therapeutic approach was her underlying belief that individual competence and autonomy were fundamental ingredients for growth and maturation. This premise provided the nucleus for a myriad of clinical intervention methods Satir designed for use with individuals, couples and families. The essence of Satir's Process Model aims toward increasing the sense of self, or self-worth, of each member within the system. The ability to stand on one's own feet was characteristic not only of Virginia Satir herself, but was also indigenous to her treatment aims.

Joan E. Winter, LCSW, is Director of the Family Institute of Virginia, 2910 Monument Avenue, Richmond, VA 23221. Leanne R. E. Parker, MEd, is Research Coordinator, Family Institute of Virginia, 2910 Monument Avenue, Richmond, VA 23221.

The authors wish to express their appreciation to Susan S. Tolson, MEd, Research Assistant, Family Institute of Virginia, for the editorial assistance she contributed to this article.

59

Accordingly, Satir's clinical approach with couples focused on the development of individual autonomy. Moreover, while strengthening and expanding independent functioning, she attempted to build a meaningful connection between the marital pair. Intrinsic to the Process Model is the interactive nature of autonomy and connection, or separateness and relatedness. However, without the vital element of individual autonomy, she observed that couples unsuccessfully attempt to obtain a sense of self from their mates.

Allied with this perspective was Satir's premise that marriage represented "the hope for a second chance" (V. Satir, personal communication, February 6, 1986). That is, the losses and disappointments in a person's childhood, particularly those experienced within the family of origin, result in an unconscious proclivity when selecting a marital partner. For example, a person who grew up with an alcoholic parent may select a mate with a similar problem. Here, the hope would be that by changing one's spouse, one could unconsciously reconcile the wounds from the family of origin. The attempt to heal childhood distress through the marital relationship becomes a driving force with couples. While this wish may not be apparent to the participants, it nevertheless has a profound influence on the quality of the marital relationship. These forces have evolved into an unconscious pattern unbeknownst to the individuals.

In order to ameliorate the impact of the family of origin on the individual, along with its accompanying repercussions on the marital relationship, Satir designed a major intervention method to access and alter the family system. The Family Reconstruction process offers a comprehensive method for attempting to heal childhood wounds. As a description of this intervention is beyond the scope of the present article, the reader is referred to Banmen, Gerber, and Gomori (1988); Nerin (1986); and Winter (1990).

Aside from the impact of family dynamics on a marriage, a couple is influenced by each partner's perception of self. The interaction resulting from the spouse's personal limitations and self perceptions can hinder the quality of the marital relationship. Seeking to enhance the individual's autonomy and self worth, as well as to enrich the couple's relationship, Satir developed another major intervention method, the Parts Party. In this approach she employed a dramatic form designed to facilitate the enactment of an individual's internal process and conflicts. This method can also be applied to marital interactions. Thus, a focus on the parts within the self, and on the interaction between each spouse's parts, is portrayed.

In essence, Satir observed that there were two primary forces affecting a person's capacity to fully function. First, the residue on the psyche from an individual's family of origin influences personal dynamics. She designed the Family Reconstruction process to provide a major intervention with regard to the individual's perception of self as a result of the family system. Second, Satir asserted that the quality of self integration a person attains significantly impacts the ability to fully function. Congruence, or the correspondence between an individual's meaning and message, is an essential aim of the model. In order to expeditiously enhance the person's own level of autonomy and integration, she developed the Parts Party. Further, Satir adapted this procedure to the couple's relationship in order to enrich each individual and the couple's bond as well.

Family Reconstruction and the Parts Party are two major intervention methods which access and alter complementary aspects of the self. In these approaches, self with family, and self with self, can be fully addressed. Furthermore, when applied in the context of a couple's relationship, the Parts Party affects self with spouse.

To delineate, a part can be viewed as a characteristic aspect or attribute of oneself. As an integral component of self, "Parts we deny are like ropes around us" (Carlock, 1986, p. 2). Accordingly,

> The goals of a Parts Party are to help a person become aware that he is made up of many different parts, get acquainted with them, understand them, and learn how to use them in an harmonious and integrated manner. (Satir & Baldwin, 1983, p. 258)

A portrayal of the parts of the self leads to increased understanding and comfort with personal issues, as well as integration and acknowledgement of the person's covert struggles in the internal sphere. In the Process Model, the purpose of the Parts Party is to foster higher self-worth, increased use of self and, with couples, an improved relationship.

While Satir ascribed to the systemic nature of families, she also focused on the system within the self. The Parts Party elucidates and brings to life an individual's own system, therapeutically focusing on the relationship of the parts within the self. Satir looked at individuals, couples and families as isomorphic yet interrelated systems. Consequently, the individual as a system, unto itself, was a forum of change as well as the familial system. Each unit was viewed as an autonomous, yet linked, system.

By adapting the Parts Party method to a couple, Satir created a vivid enactment of what each person brings to the self, and to the relationship. The Couples Parts Party allows the marital pair to: *see* that which exists within the self; *learn* how those elements interact with the spouse's; *observe* how the different aspects of each partner simultaneously impact one another and; *transform* previously dysfunctional interaction between the couple into a more appreciative and understanding relationship pattern.

An overview of the Parts Party, including its underlying principles and a delineation of related theories, provides the framework for understanding an application of this approach with couples. An explication of Satir's assumptions regarding couples is followed by a summary of the implementation aspects for a Parts Party. Next, treatment implications for the Parts Party within the marital context are described. For the purposes of this article, a brief description for implementing a Parts Party is presented. With an understanding of Satir's underlying theory, its antecedents, and a description of the marital relationship, a foundation is provided for integrating Satir's Parts Party methodology with couples.

UNDERLYING PRINCIPLES

Satir observed that life consists of experiences from birth to death, which result in feelings and interpretations about those experiences. It is from such events, with their concomitant feelings and interpretations, that a person's parts begin to develop. Over time, experiences, and their subsequent interpretations, start to emerge into customary responses resulting in characteristic patterns of that individual. Carlock noted that, "these habit patterns then cluster to form personality traits and finally become crystallized into a particular pattern or structure of behaving, a personality style'' (1989, p. 4). A personal integration of an experience, with its attendant interpretation, results in the characteristic attributes or patterns of an individual, culminating in the emergence of parts.

As a consequence of the interpretation of experience, which is a necessary component for the development of parts, either a positive or negative connotation is given to a part by the individual. For example, according to Satir and Baldwin (1983), anger is often viewed as a negative part of the self. Early in life the child may have absorbed messages about the expression of anger being unacceptable or dangerous. A developmental process generally unfolds in the following four part sequence:

1. A child expresses anger and is scolded (*experience*).
2. The child translates the experience into the perception that anger is "bad" (*interpretation*).
3. Repeated experiences of this nature produce a learning model that interprets anger as unacceptable (*pattern*).
4. Recurrent manifestation that anger is a problematic pattern leads to a characteristic response and an internal embodiment of the experience (*part*).

Thus, parts naturally emerge in a successive manner: *experience* → *interpretation* → *pattern* → *part*. A Parts Party begins by focusing on the final aspect in this sequence, the part itself. Also, it aims toward influencing each aspect of a part's developmental process, including pattern, interpretation and experience. In a Couples Parts Party, the focus expands to address both spouse's parts, as well as the interaction between them.

In the case of a negatively perceived part, the person begins to deny the existence of the feelings that would lead to expression of the disowned emotion. On the other hand, a part that is valued and embraced by an individual becomes increasingly apparent in the person's repertoire of responses. An overdependence on the so-called positive part may result in less personal flexibility and masked vulnerability. This process is further exacerbated in the relationship between a couple. In this context, one partner may value a particular aspect of their spouse and dislike another part. As such preferences become known, either directly or indirectly, another potent force in shaping the expression of each partner evolves. In this manner, aspects of each mate and the core of the marriage is affected. That is, the partners are constricted in the expression of aspects of the self through two dimensions. First, if a part is valued by the spouse, it is reinforced and may be excessively relied upon within the marriage. On the other hand, if a part is considered unacceptable its expression may be curtailed. Therefore, the self of each spouse is profoundly shaped by the interaction of the marital system.

Due to the wealth of experiences of each individual, there are many and varied parts, with each part having a need for fulfillment. All parts, in essence, provide a protective function for the individuals. Each has evolved due to its survival value for the self. A part's protective nature is revealed during the course of the party, which in turn can reframe a negative connotation. In this manner, the benefits of reclaiming and honoring disowned parts are experienced by the individual.

The Parts Party's lively enactment of the internal sphere serves to make aspects of the self palpable. Likewise, with a couple, each person has an opportunity to observe the functional aspect of their mate's patterns of relating. This, then, can lead to accessibility and understanding of the protective nature of one another's parts, and how different parts may effectively work together to increase the individual and couple's flexibility. As the part is reframed, such that its negative connotation is transformed, and its function is fully understood, integration is more likely to follow for both the individual and the couple. Recognition that purported "good parts," taken to extreme, can have detrimental consequences, and that "negative parts" have preserving and protective elements, is a fundamental objective of the Parts Party.

Parts also carry energy, or an impelling force, within the individual. Energy represents an inherent power or capacity to take action or to resist expression. The fuel source for energy derives from feelings. Acknowledging the existence of the feelings frees the energy. As in the manifestation of a positively perceived part, energy is willingly invested to express the desirable part. On the other hand, for negatively viewed parts, an effort to curtail the energy is attempted. Satir observed that people divide their "parts into good and bad" (Satir & Banmen, 1983, p. 518). Nevertheless, she asserted that energy exists within all parts and that "the energy is either allowed to flow out" or "it acts like a hungry dog that you're not feeding, and it's starting to get an itch. And the manifestation of an itch can be in some kind of illness . . . or interactional destructiveness . . . the energy goes angry" (p. 518). Accordingly, she emphasized that "energy is never killed . . . it only gets transformed" (p. 518).

Transformation, which in its broadest scope implies a change in an external form, inner nature, or function, is an intrinsic component within the Satir Process Model. Utilizing the original elements of experience, interpretation, pattern, and part, the transformation process attempts to convert the existing energy into a more viable and functional form. As indicated, reframing facilitates conversion of a person's, as well as a couple's, perspective. Transformation furthers the process by metamorphosing the original nature of an object, or part, into a more suitable or desirable form. To illustrate, the Hans Christian Andersen fairy tale, describing the transformation of an ugly duckling into a swan, epitomizes the therapeutic process in a Parts Party. Unlike the duckling's gradual alteration, the catalytic nature of the Parts Party was designed by Satir to illustrate, and consequently hasten, the metaphorical integration of the individual's parts.

Satir and Baldwin also underscored the importance of the individual believing that choices, and the potential of cooperation between different parts, exist in the expression of a part:

> Every part carries an aspect of energy which serves to transform it when it understands that it has choices in how and when to manifest itself and that it can cooperate with other parts rather than fighting with them. (1983, p. 259)

Thus, two essential ingredients for the expression of a part are the context in which a part manifests itself, as well as the possibility of cooperation with other parts of the self. Additionally, both context and cooperation are relevant in the expression of parts within the couple's relationship. This includes cooperation among parts of each self, as well as the collaboration among the spouses' parts.

Context within Satir theory represents the situation in which an interaction takes place. *Context* represents one of the three dimensions of interaction within the Satir model, along with the dimensions of *self* and *other*. The contextual component of a part's expression is an important consideration in a Parts Party. Additionally, cooperation between varying parts contributes to the process of being able to manifest all of an individual's parts, both separately and within the marital relationship. When each individual within a marriage is fully aware of the existence and possible contribution of all parts within the self and the spouse, selection of a viable context enables expression of the part.

As a result, there are parts of the self that are embraced and welcomed fully; they are honored and expressed often. In general, these aspects supply the bridge between the self and other, thereby diminishing the individual's existential sense of aloneness. There are other parts that are not valued, and therefore denied; these are useful, but their purpose may be obscured. Once transformed, these extruded parts provide a valuable self-protective umbrella under which the person may experience a sense of inner security. Finally, there are parts that are seemingly unknown, which are yet to be discovered by the individual. These unfamiliar aspects enhance the individual's potential for maturation and growth. These expressions of an individual's parts are also inherent in the interaction between the couple.

The Couples Parts Party attempts to surface these valued, alienated, extruded and unknown aspects of each partner and reframe them so that they can be reclaimed by the individual and expressed within the relationship. According to Satir, such a resolution increases the level of functioning for both the self and allied systems, including the marital, familial, and collegial systems. Ultimately, higher self-worth results when a person is able to lay claim to all parts, validating their existence and embracing the self such as it is. Further, a similar expression of self within the couple's relationship positively contributes to marital quality.

The parallel theoretical antecedents of Parts Parties are overviewed in the next section. This is followed by an explication of

Satir's assumptions regarding couples and a description of the requisite elements for implementation of a Couples Parts Party.

PARALLEL THEORETICAL RATIONALES

Components of Jungian, Gestalt, psychodrama, hypnosis and family systems theory parallel aspects of Satir's Parts Party. According to Carlock, "the roots of the Parts Party lie in numerous theories" (1986, p. 3). This section describes and amplifies corresponding theoretical rationales that intersect with Satir theory which guides the Parts Party.

Two diverse conceptual frameworks which describe the development of a self, or the process of individuation, are closely allied to Satir's approach as applied in Parts Parties. There is a theoretical correspondence with Jungian (Jung, 1973) and Gestalt theory (Perls, 1969; Polster & Polster, 1973; Zinker, 1977) in Satir's approach to the self. While Satir developed her methodology independent of these theories, there is a common ground between these models with regard to the understanding and development of the self.

In Jung's model, developing a sense of "psychological wholeness," or integration of the various aspects of the self, is primary. Jung's examination and explication of archetypes focused on the integration of parts within the self.

In a related vein, Gestalt theorists have also emphasized the integration of polarities within the self, or, those aspects of a person that seem necessarily to be at odds and incapable of residing peacefully together within the individual. For example, the duality of assertiveness and passivity represent one such polarity. As indicated, Satir observed (Satir & Banmen, 1983) that often one of these polarities was seen by an individual as good, while the other was viewed as bad, contributing to the internal conflict regarding the part's use and expression. This process is also affected by each mate's view of the partner's polarities. Gestalt theory contains a fundamental premise that a person needs to incorporate the diverse polarities of the self, including those parts which are alienated due to their perceived undesirability. In the Satir approach, discovering and incorporating existing, or perhaps simply unknown or dormant parts, contribute to psychological wholeness, or the gestalt of the person. Further, within the couple, incorporating diverse differences is crucial to enhancing the vitality of the relationship.

As previously explicated, Satir viewed individuals, couples and families as isomorphic yet interrelated systems. Her treatment of family systems, as a whole unit, preceded the development of the Parts Party intervention. Consequently, there are a number of elements of systems theory that permeate her approach to individuals. The linkages between the individual, marital and family system are apparent in the theory and application of Parts Parties.

There is a recognition in family systems theory of the interrelatedness of all family members. That is, it is not one family member that solely creates a dysfunctional system, rather it is the interrelationship of the members and their consequent patterns of interaction. Likewise, in the individual, one alienated aspect of the self is not the "rotten apple" that the person must extrude in order to attain happiness. As in a family system, where there are "no good guys and bad guys" (Carlock, 1986, p. 5), in a Parts Party there are no good guys or bad guys within the individual system. Hence, it is an illusion that there are entirely constructive or destructive representative aspects of the self. A Parts Party attempts to tease out individual aspects of a person so that the patterns, interrelatedness and mutual influences of parts become apparent to both the individual and the couple.

In a closed marital or family system it is not uncommon for the members' roles to become rigid and narrow. According to systems theory, as individuals become defined and labelled by such roles, the ability to express self and grow in any way but the prescribed manner is limited. The role assumed may be different from that which the person believes is congruent with the true self. Similarly, parts within an individual may also be so identified and labelled. The manner in which a part is perceived affects its expression. Rigidifying of parts may proscribe vital aspects of the self. In the family system roles rigidify; in the individual system parts become inflexible. Parts can be transformed so that their unique contributions to the wholeness of an individual and the couple become viable. Marital and family therapy utilizing the Satir Process Model attempts to surface the possibilities for all members of a system.

Discovering how constricting and suffocating a label can be is another aim of this treatment approach. The Parts Party parallels this discovery process by reframing an individual's perception of self.

On another dimension, the Parts Party accesses the individual's sensory experiences. The capacity to perceive self and environment from a variety of dimensions is innate to human beings. Maximum use of the person's sensory abilities remains a hallmark of Satir's treatment methods. Similarly, Carlock noted that Gestalt theory's "emphasis on sensation as the raw data of our experience" (1986, p. 7) is consistent with the practices of a Parts Party. Bodily perceptions and sensations of participants are an informative source of data and are attended to by the therapist. Initial reactions to the enactment portrayed in a Parts Party register in the body, and it is from this source that clues to the individual or couple's experience are derived. The body, as a primary data source, is fundamental to both the Gestalt and Satir treatment approaches.

With regard to hypnosis, the personification of parts in the context of a party induces a trance-like state (Carlock, 1989). As a person begins to view aspects of the self in a dramatic form, externalized on the basis of one's own private internal reality, a hypnotic dissociation occurs. Trance, being an altered state of awareness, is naturally induced in this manner.

Further, as the person absorbs in a sensory form elements of the self, a change in consciousness occurs. Taking information in on a variety of levels, the unconscious is quickly accessed in a Parts Party. Satir valued the hypnotic quality of the right brain for its powerful sensory input, "because the right brain doesn't understand one thing about words, it only understands pictures and sounds and touches" (Satir & Banmen, 1983, p. 577).

Finally, Moreno's pioneering effort in developing psychodrama as a therapeutic intervention provides another parallel theoretical model to the Parts Party. According to Carlock, "the use of role-players to enact various parts of the personality is a method which has its roots in psychodrama (Moreno, 1977). Enactment is a way of blending the cognitive and the experiential" (1989, p. 10). Once again, a Parts Party is a method that directly accesses the right side of the brain. Further, by virtue of the rational and explicit specification of the parts, the left side of the brain is also tapped.

It is with this foundation that a Parts Party is envisioned. Understanding the theoretical basis of this method provides a framework for applying the Parts Party within a therapeutic context for couples.

SATIR'S PERSPECTIVE
REGARDING COUPLES

In the Process Model Satir formulated a number of premises regarding couples. The capacity to maintain autonomy and relatedness is central to this approach. Satir's theoretical assumptions serve as a foundation for clinical interventions with couples, including the Parts Party. The following synopsis presents Satir's perspective on couples.

As indicated, the fundamental task of each individual is to attain a sense of competence and autonomy. Satir observed that love cannot carry all the demands of life. Nor can love be the sole source of happiness. From her perspective, "intelligence, information, awareness and competence" were vital elements contributing to individual satisfaction (Satir, 1988, p. 142). Indeed, Satir stated, "The single most crucial factor in love relationships is the feeling of worth each person has for self" (p. 145). The capacity of each member of the relationship to "stand on their own two feet," being responsible for self, is essential to what Satir termed "positive pairing" (p. 325).

When a marital relationship is based on a survival pact, where each partner attempts to borrow a sense of self from the mate, difficulties are inevitable. In such a case, Satir illustrated the marital dialogue in this manner: "If I run out of supplies I will take from you. You will have enough, in an emergency, to serve us both" (1967, p. 9). Autonomy is not feasible within such a dysfunctional pact because it threatens the homeostasis of the marital bond. Since the spouses believe that their very survival is dependent on their partner, individuation is seriously hampered.

Furthermore, the selection of a mate is a complex and, at one level, unconscious process. As indicated, the wounds of childhood are recapitulated in the marital relationship. These dynamics may surface by selecting a partner with similar, unresolved issues as those lived through in the family of origin. Or, paradoxically, the choice of a spouse may represent the perceived opposite dynamics from the family of origin. This oppositional strategy essentially culminates in the same result. Either way, the individual is unduly influenced in mate selection by old familial scars and the "hope for a second chance."

Moreover, how mates are chosen provides an essential clue regarding current marital disappointment and dysfunction. Don Jackson (1968), a mentor of Satir's, hypothesized that if a clinician knew how a couple first met, a reliable prediction of their current problems could be advanced. Satir translated this notion into her frequent inquiry in family sessions, "How did you two first lay eyes on one another?" Another variation on this theme was her question, "Out of all the people in the world, what was it about this person that made you feel, 'this is the one for me?'" The identification of initial hopes, dreams and wishes for the marital relationship was employed by Satir as both a diagnostic and treatment tool.

Satir asserted that mate selection was "not an accident" (1967, p. 8). Aside from an attempt to heal childhood wounds by replacing the alleged "bad parent" with a "good parent" (p. 10), she hypothesized that spouses hope their mate will also fill in qualities which are believed to be missing in the self. For example, if the person perceives the self as deficient in being logical or rational, those qualities in a mate may be viewed as a desirable complement to the self. From this perspective, the misguided idea is that two halves will make a whole. The problem with this belief, however, is that a successful marriage requires two whole, autonomous individuals as a basis for fulfillment. While autonomy is a necessary prerequisite for marital functioning, in this model it is not a sufficient condition for happiness.

Accordingly, Satir (1988) observed that there are three systems operating among couples. She described these parts as "you, me, and us." From this perspective, each component is equally significant, each system possessing an energy force of its own. The development of these three respective aspects of a couple make the other components more functional. Thus, as each system is nurtured, the other parts are promoted, each directly benefitting from its own development, and indirectly from the growth of the other two components. In Satir's model, effort expended toward solidifying you, me, and us, the three interlinked systems, enhances the quality of the marriage. The Couples Parts Party is designed to enable change in these autonomous yet related systems.

The manner in which these three aspects of a couple interact establishes, in part, the process between the marital pair. In Satir's model the evolution of an effective process between family members is a primary aim. Process is a systemic method or a way of doing something. According to Satir, process is consistently employed in everyday decision-making that occurs between people. Considering that process is of critical importance in a relationship, Satir noted that, "Love is the feeling that begins a marriage, but it is the day-to-day living—their process—that will determine how the marriage works" (1988, p. 145). Satir observed that marriage is similar to a corporation: "whether it succeeds depends on its organization, the 'how' of its endeavors, its process" (p. 151). She continued, "Probably nothing is so vital to developing and maintaining a love relationship (or killing it) as . . . process" (p. 148).

An emphasis on the development of effective process skills is characteristic of Satir's treatment approach. The ability to listen to the other, take in what is said and simultaneously be aware of one's own thoughts and feelings is essential. Remaining open to hearing and integrating the other person's perspective, yet in touch with the self, is vital to the development of a productive process. The importance of process within this model cannot be understated. A Satir maxim was, "it's not the problem, it's the process." How people cope with problems, as opposed to the specific content of the issues, provides the quintessential element for change within the Satir model.

The Parts Party helps to create the process occurring between a couple. When process can be illuminated and enhanced, it becomes increasingly possible for a couple to grow beyond the pain, disappointment and misunderstandings that emerge in all marriages. Accordingly, as an effective process evolves, feelings of love become more apparent within a relationship. When a couple has developed a functional process between them they can handle the challenges life inevitably brings, knowing they can, indeed, depend on one another yet not be smothered.

Beyond the marital dyad, the couple sets the definitive tone for how the family functions. Satir maintained that the marital pair are the "architects of the family" (1967, p. 1). Thus, the relationship dynamics between the husband and wife form the base and blueprint of each family's structure. Satir observed that the hopes for marriage are those from the heart, yet the capacity to think things through impacts the couple's process. "Many people regard the heart as weak. They think only the head is strong. We forget that good architecture requires both: we can design relationships that function and that please us as well" (Satir, 1988, p. 143).

Family architecture requires both "love and process" (Satir, 1988, p. 150) in order to sustain the family system. The cultivation of a productive marital process is affected by several factors. Integration of diverse parts of the self impacts upon the capacity to sustain an effective marital process. Furthermore, the residue of deficits from the family of origin affects each partner's ability to connect and simultaneously maintain autonomy within the marital bond.

The family of origin is the incubator for an individual's sense of self worth. According to Winter and Aponte (1987), another way of conceptualizing this dynamic is that the family of origin becomes the *unit of identity*. In this milieu a personal perception of self is formed. On the other hand, the family of procreation becomes the *unit of healing*. Within the marriage the desire to mend and grow flourishes as a result of the deficits in one or both partners. Oftentimes this wish remains unfilled. In such instances, neither partner, alone or together, possesses the capacity to initiate and sustain a restoration process. Nevertheless, the hope for healing remains a potent force within the marital context. Frequently the partners are able to contribute, separately and together, toward the development of meaningful autonomy and connection.

While the marital relationship can be a potent force in change, when the spouse's level of competence and autonomy is proscribed, the relationship is also limited in its ability to sustain a positive direction. Satir observed that when a system gets stuck, one of three possibilities emerge: someone can die; someone can leave; or there can be an intervention (Winter, 1990). The introduction of a foreign element into a dysfunctional system becomes the change agent.

Thus, if the marital unit is unable to cope with sustained stress, an external resource can enter the system and become a catalyst for change.

The autonomy and maturity of each partner is a critical variable in the quality of a marital relationship. According to Satir, a person possessing a higher sense of self esteem expects less continual concrete evidence of self worth from the spouse. On the other hand, those with an impaired perception of self esteem make greater demands on the spouse. As a consequence, those with low self esteem generally have relationships with distinct characteristics. Here, the individual wants the partner's validation to compensate for the diminished perception of self. As indicated, the spouse is perceived as having qualities that are believed to be lacking in the self, therefore, the mate becomes a psychological extension of self, a way of attempting to make oneself whole. According to Satir, each partner has high hopes about what to expect from the other, yet simultaneously also possesses great fears, anticipating disappointment. What emerges from this pattern is a general sense of distrust between the two.

When each partner attempts this dysfunctional extension of self, needing approval from the other, differences and dissatisfaction with one another and the relationship are inevitably avoided. In this context, acknowledged dissimilarities might lead to disagreement and conflict. According to Satir, "Fighting means anger; anger means death. So to live, avoid differentness" (1988, p. 155). In addition, each individual is reminded that the other is not an extension of self, but a separate entity. A disagreement means the loss of the self that is defined by the other.

By ignoring differentness in the self and the partner, there is a pseudo melding of the two people. On the surface, each has given control of the self to the other. While each has unconsciously accepted the responsibility for supplementing the self esteem of the partner, there is an underlying resentment of this duty. By allowing the other to define one's self worth a vulnerability evolves. The sense of self no longer exists within the individual. Rather, it has been given to the other, and what has been given can also be taken away. Moreover, the uniqueness of each self does not evaporate, it simply manifests itself covertly in order to maintain the appearance of sameness between the two individuals.

Satir acknowledged that this striving to uphold pseudo-sameness, by ignoring those qualities in the other that are disliked or different from self, cannot last forever. "When two people are together, the chances of them meeting each other's faces over time are 100 percent" (Satir & Banmen, 1983, p. 545). Thus, the various parts of each self are known to the spouse, both consciously and unconsciously. Given time, threats to the appearance of sameness will inevitably be encountered, as all parts of the self, including those unacknowledged or different from the spouse, will manifest.

Satir asserted that there is a myth that "love means sameness" (1988, p. 154). While she acknowledged that two people initially become interested in each other because of their sameness, "they remain interested over the years because of their ability to enjoy differences" (p. 154). In essence, differences exude an aura of mystery. In the mature couple, differences have the capacity to generate excitement within the marriage. The congruent pair will seek to discover differences early in the relationship. In this manner, they are challenged to explore ways to deal constructively with differences, rather than struggling against them. Further, an appreciation of the mystique inherent to each mate, or that part of the other that is not completely known, is preserved.

The Couples Parts Party is designed to facilitate a process of constructively working with differences between the marital pair. As spouses observe the enactment of their differentness, they become aware of new possibilities. When differences are acknowledged and the energy contained within that part is freed, an integral part of self and other can be accepted. Consequently, higher self esteem can develop.

The recognition and incorporation of individual parts, separate and distinct from the mate, also fosters autonomy. As indicated, autonomy is a vital component each individual has the capacity to contribute to the relationship. By virtue of the Parts Party itself, where each part is given its own name and individualized description, the partners naturally initiate the process of recognizing, understanding and accepting differentness.

Valuing oneself, as well as the other, while being responsible for self, is a central factor in Satir's approach with couples. Satir delineated eight ingredients in a "positive pairing relationship." These include:

1. Each person stands firmly on his or her own feet and is autonomous.
2. Each person can be counted on to say real "yes's" and "no's" — in other words, to be emotionally honest.
3. Each person can ask for what she or he wants.
4. Each acknowledges and takes responsibility for her or his actions.
5. Each can keep promises.
6. Each can be counted on to be kind, fun to be around, courteous, considerate, and real.
7. Each takes full freedom to choose to comment on what is going on.
8. Each supports the other's dreams in whatever way possible. Together, they cooperate instead of competing. (1988, p. 332)

An awareness of these aspects of a paired relationship is vital to understanding Satir's intervention approach with couples. Her theoretical assumptions regarding functional relationships build a foundation for the utilization of a Couples Parts Party. Since Satir viewed the partner's relationship as "the axis around which all other family relationships are formed" (1967, p. 1), its importance within the family system can hardly be underrated. The Parts Party serves to plant the seeds of a more constructive, loving relationship, in which differences between the spouses are embraced and viewed as a challenge within the marriage.

APPLICATION

The implementation of a Couples Parts Party may take a number of different forms, depending on the individuals and the physical resources at hand. According to Satir and Baldwin, "To be meaningful, techniques need to be tailor-made for the situation" (1983,

p. 241). However, certain characteristics of a Parts Party are universal. This section will briefly describe the customary elements in the application of a Parts Party. The following overviews the fundamental components of the Parts Party process and provides a foundation for implementation of the method with couples.

Preparatory Stage

A Parts Party requires: approximately 3 to 4 hours; a *Host*, that is, client or person whose party it is; a *Guide*, the therapist or facilitator for the party; and a minimum of six other people, preferably 8 to 10. These participants are termed the *Guests*, who play the parts and attend the gathering.

Prior to the party, the Host is asked to select six well-known people who symbolize either a personal attraction or repulsion. In determining the selection of parts, Satir often asked, "Who makes your hair stand on end, who makes you juicy?" (Satir & Banmen, 1983, p. 519). Satir also observed that invited parts "all live in the mind of the one having the party" (p. 520). Thus, the selection of one's parts is a distinctly personal choice, one that cannot be determined by anyone else, including the spouse.

It is essential that a Parts Party have at least one unsavory character, in order to surface the polarities within the individual. The importance of representing the extremes within the self results from early childhood experiences. Generally, people remember being encouraged to "Be good." In the child's mind, the extremes of good and bad became evident. Good was to be desired and bad to be denied. The heart of a Parts Party is the transformation of these perceived polarities within the self, and their subsequent ownership and integration within the Host. With couples, recognition and acceptance of each other's parts is an additional aim.

Another aspect of the preparatory stage is the Host's choice of an adjective to describe each part. Further, a delineation of whether the attribute is viewed as negative or positive is requested. This facilitates an understanding of the person's view of self. At times, Satir would ask for a "switch." That is, if a trait was viewed as a positive attribute, she might have asked the Host to, "Tell me some time when it would be negative" (Satir & Banmen, 1983, p. 521). This process subtly begins to reframe a part, planting a seed that aspects of the self can have at least two purposes, both positive and negative. Thus, the consideration of new possibilities emerges.

Satir advised the Host to "use your radar" (Satir & Banmen, 1983, p. 521) when selecting participants to enact the parts. This choice is not envisioned as a systematic process. Thus, the selection of parts is considered a more intuitive, unconscious process. In this manner, the right brain is activated, which in turn makes a significant contribution to both the party and the process of integration.

Another means of tapping the right brain results from the use of props and costumes, augmenting the senses of sight and sound. By selecting parts prior to the party, the Guests have an opportunity to organize appropriate attire, thus enhancing the impact of the party.

Additionally, the creative efforts of the parts adds a humorous element, contributing to a party-like atmosphere. The inherent fun of people coming together, dressed in costumes or using props, portraying famous persons with certain characteristics, is integral to new perceptions and learning. The incorporation of fun overlaps with the intense nature of so vividly seeing internal struggles played out. The threatening aspect of sharing such intimate clashes is lessened. Satir valued the therapeutic effects of merriment and stated, "I do my most definitive and serious work when the atmosphere is light" (1988, p. 228). Furthermore, props, sound effects and costumes provide a dramatic manifestation of the "movie that you have never seen before, only felt" (Satir & Banmen, 1983, p. 522).

The preparatory stage, which precedes the actual Parts Party, maximizes the benefit of the method. When planning commences prior to the event, the Host engages in a prolonged consideration of aspects of the self and the meaning ascribed to each of the parts. In reality, a Parts Party begins at the moment a person commits to participating in the enactment. Further, since a number of people and resources are utilized during the party, their contribution is expedited and enhanced by advance planning. As a result, the impact of the intervention is expanded for both the Host and the participants.

Party Stage

The party itself begins as the Guests start to interact. In a Couples Parts Party, the parts of each mate converse with one another, dramatizing their interactions and everyday exchanges. In this manner, it becomes possible to view dysfunctional, as well as tender and delightful encounters. Vulnerable parts become apparent, and a process for creating a sense of security for these aspects of self evolves.

An important component resulting from the visual aspect of the party is the bodily impact the Host experiences while observing interactions among the parts. The familiarity of conflicts, and productive interactions, becomes evident and physically registers in the body. Thus, feelings and bodily sensations provide essential clues to individual perceptions. These sensations lead to an increased awareness and recognition of intrapersonal and interpersonal issues. Exploration of these perceptions contributes to the integration of the parts at the end of the party.

Another aspect of the Parts Party focuses on understanding how different parts coming together can act both constructively and destructively. By observing how parts connect and disconnect, reflecting flexibility and rigidity within each spouse, the couple is enlightened about their interactive process. Witnessing one's life portrayed on a stage deeply affects both partners. Such viewing of relationship dynamics initiates the transformation of parts. As parts are transformed, it becomes tenable to see new possibilities and resources both in the self and the mate. Transformation enables revision in the encounters played out between the partners. In this manner, the selection of a viable context conducive to future interactions is facilitated. Parts also learn ways to cooperate and help each other, contributing once again to the ultimate integration of all parts.

With increased understanding and cooperation within the couple's relationship, additional choices emerge. An expanded awareness of acceptance, trust and security with regard to both the self and the other occurs. As a result, each partner can begin to express wishes, dreams and yearnings for the relationship that had become dormant. Similarly, alienated, extruded or unknown aspects of the self can be claimed. Renewed hope that the future can indeed be different follows. At this point, there begins to be a therapeutic, or changed quality to the marital dynamics.

The Couples Parts Party clearly identifies aspects of both the self and the partner that easily and effectively interact. By discovering those parts that connect, as well as those that clash, a couple can consciously choose which distinct components can be employed to enhance the quality of their communication. This identification may help the couple in future interactions to remember that there can be enhanced possibilities for growth and cooperation through the joining of certain parts.

This overview of a Couples Parts Party describes only rudimentary elements common to the application of the method. The specifics of conducting a Parts Party are beyond the scope of this article. For further amplification of the techniques employed in a Parts Party, the reader is referred to Banmen, Gerber, and Gomori (1988); Carlock (1986, 1989); Satir and Banmen (1983); and Winter (1990).

Many variations on the Parts Party theme are possible, depending on the time available, context, and accessible people. New and unforeseen applications of a Parts Party await only the curiosity and creativity of the therapist. Satir tailored every party to fit individual and contextual considerations. However, an understanding of the general course of a Parts Party serves to amplify the underlying theory and the implications for treatment.

IMPLICATIONS FOR TREATMENT

The Process Model's hypotheses about the marital relationship provide a variety of implications for treatment. Similar to Bowen's position which aims toward developing a more differentiated self (Bowen, 1978), Satir emphasized the importance of personal competence and autonomy. This aim is a fundamental goal of both Satir and Bowen Theory. While these pioneers have developed distinct methods of achieving this goal, it remains a common theoretical assumption in each model.

Among other techniques, Satir developed the Couples Parts Party in order to surface and intervene within the three essential components of the couple: self, other and relationship. This process can be employed within a group context, or can be adapted to a marital or individual treatment milieu, utilizing a gestalt imagery process. In either case, the therapist has a diverse repertoire for both thinking and intervening within a marital dyad.

Practitioners aspiring to utilize the Parts Party methodology in their own context need clinical training for both the requisite technical and personal skills. The process itself is complex and necessitates supervised practice in order to develop competence. Further, Satir asserted that an application of such methods to one's own life benefits the person of the therapist and, generally, should be undertaken before attempting to implement the intervention with others. The integration of self achieved through a Parts Party and Family Reconstruction enhances the therapist's technical skills.

CONCLUSION

Virginia Satir's Parts Party proved to be one of her most innovative and influential techniques for effecting change, both intrapersonally and interpersonally. The opportunity to view an externalization of one's internal process opens the door for a greater understanding and acceptance of self. Integration of one's parts is a fundamental and requisite component of the change process. Further, the addition of a spouse, who is also attempting to consolidate aspects of the self, augments the benefits of the intervention.

The Couples Parts Party is designed to enhance the autonomous functioning of each spouse, as well as provide a bridge within their relationship. A change in any one of these systems affects the other two systems. This intervention simultaneously accesses both the left and right brain, further amplifying its impact. The therapist can employ the methodology with a number of variations, depending upon the context. Acceptance of self leads to increased competence and autonomy, culminating in higher self-worth. As each mate's self-esteem is raised, the link between them becomes more genuine and solid. The culmination of these efforts enhances congruent communication, surfaces each person's yearnings, and awakens the couple's hopes and dreams.

REFERENCES

Banmen, J., Gerber, J., & Gomori, M. (1988). *The Virginia Satir growth model: A study guide on becoming more fully human.* (Available from Delta Psychological Services, 11213 Canyon Crescent, N. Delta, British Columbia, Canada V4E 2R6).

Bowen, M. (1978). *Family therapy in clinical practice.* New York: Jason Aronson.

Carlock, C. J. (1986). *The Parts Party for self-concept: Differentiation and integration.* Unpublished manuscript.

Carlock, C. J. (1989). *The Parts Party for self-concept: Differentiation and integration.* Manuscript submitted for publication in V. Satir & J. Banmen (Eds.), *The Satir system and impact.* Palo Alto, CA: Science and Behavior Books.

Jackson, D. D. (Ed.). (1968). Communication, family, and marriage. (Vol. 1. *Human Communication*). Palo Alto, CA: Science and Behavior Books.

Jung, C. J. (1973). *Mandala Symbolism.* Princeton, NJ: Princeton University Press.

Moreno, J. L. (1977). *Psychodrama* (Vol. 1, 4th ed.). Beacon, NY: Beacon House.

Nerin, W. F. (1986). *Family reconstruction: Long day's journey into light.* New York: W. W. Norton.

Perls, F. S. (1969). *Gestalt therapy verbatim.* Lafayette, CA: Real People Press.

Polster, F., & Polster, M. (1973). *Gestalt therapy integrated: Contours of theory and practice.* New York: Brunner/Mazel.

Satir, V. (1967). *Conjoint family therapy.* Palo Alto, CA: Science and Behavior Books.

Satir, V. (1988). *The new peoplemaking.* Palo Alto, CA: Science and Behavior Books.

Satir, V., & Baldwin, M. (1983). *Satir step by step.* Palo Alto, CA: Science and Behavior Books.

Satir, V., & Banmen, J. (1983). *Virginia Satir verbatim 1984.* (Available from Delta Psychological Services, 11213 Canyon Crescent, N. Delta, British Columbia, Canada, V4E 2R6.)

Winter, J. E. (1990). *Family research project: Family therapy outcome study of Bowen, Haley, and Satir.* Unpublished manuscript.

Winter, J. E., & Aponte, H. (1987). The family life of psychotherapists: Treatment and training implications. In F. W. Kaslow (Ed.), *The family life of psychotherapists: Clinical implications* (pp. 97-133). New York: Haworth Press.

Zinker, J. (1977). *Creative process in gestalt therapy.* New York: Brunner/Mazel.

Increasing Couple Intimacy Using Virginia Satir's Temperature Reading

Lynne M. Azpeitia
Walter F. Zahnd

SUMMARY. This article describes the process of using Virginia Satir's Temperature Reading, a communication tool, to increase intimacy with couples. It presents a rationale and theory for using a daily couple Temperature Reading to develop communication skills for learning how to share intimately in relationships. Temperature Reading provides a safe environment where each member of the couple can learn to share personal information and can practice listening to the other in a supportive and cooperative manner. Therapists and couples alike can utilize this process as described here.

The more full and complete the contact that we make with ourselves and each other, the more possible it is to feel loved and valued, to be healthy and to learn how to be more effective in solving our problems. (Satir, 1976, p.1)

Nowhere is the universal human yearning to be loved and appreciated more visible than in today's couple relationships. Virginia Satir's Temperature Reading is a communication tool that couples can use on their own to experience, develop and increase their level of intimacy. While Temperature Reading was originally developed

Lynne M. Azpeitia, MA, member, Virginia Satir's Avanta Network, is Professor of Family Therapy and Director of Interns, California Family Study Center, 5433 Laurel Canyon Blvd., North Hollywood, CA 91607. Walter F. Zahnd, MSW, member, Virginia Satir's Avanta Network, is Professor, Department of Sociology and Social Work, California State University, Chico, CA 95969.

for use in a group or family (Satir, 1988), it is an excellent vehicle for fostering close and intimate sharing in couple relationships. A couple Temperature Reading consists of the practice of setting aside a time period daily for making contact and reconnecting with each other. The use of Temperature Reading provides a fully human context where couples can feel what they feel, say what they feel and think, ask for what they want, and take risks in their own behalf (Satir, 1976). Doing this enhances communication and raises self esteem.

In all forms of couple relationships the use of Temperature Reading provides a safe environment where each member of the couple can learn to share personal information and can practice listening to the other in a supportive and cooperative manner. It facilitates the open sharing of the whole human being so that a close human connection can take place. In an effective and non-threatening way, it surfaces and addresses the overt and covert issues which are present in couple relationships. It legitimizes feelings and brings into awareness many things people have learned to keep to themselves. It provides a healthy process for maintaining open lines of couple communication.

Research has shown that openly communicating and intimately connecting with your partner on a continuous basis is one of the most important ingredients in successful coupling (Gottman, 1982; Thomas, Albrecht & White, 1984; Tuites & Tuites, 1986; Wampler, 1982; Zimmer, 1983). The ongoing practice of sharing, receiving and affirming each individual's personal experience is positively correlated with marital satisfaction, health and longevity. Developing and integrating this practice of talking freely with and listening fully to your partner is the single most consistent ingredient listed in article after article on successful coupling (Dinkmeyer & Carlson, 1986; Napier, 1988; Stone and Winkelman, 1990; Satir, 1988; Solomon, 1989; Welwood; 1985). These communication skills, which are so necessary to the vitality of each person and the marriage, must be learned and used if the relationship is to become and remain intimate. There is no substitute for this.

As every experienced couples therapist knows, the majority of couples do not begin their relationships equipped with these skills (Beck, 1988). Most of us have not yet learned how to clearly and congruently communicate our innermost feelings, thoughts, perceptions, expectations and yearnings. We come out of our family of origin experiences knowing more about how to protect our vulnerable self than how to share it. In part, this is the result of the childhood decisions we made about what to share of our thoughts, feelings and self. When these early survival rules are activated in adulthood to protect, conceal or hide the vulnerable or unacceptable parts of ourselves, they do little to help us know and understand ourselves and each other. In fact, these family learnings can prove damaging because they increasingly restrict the areas of a person's unique self that can be shared freely with his/her partner. Intimacy cannot take place between people when they are engaged more in efforts to hide themselves than to reveal themselves. These emotional rules need to change before we can do what we need to in order to live intimately with another person. A large part of effective coupling requires the transformation of these rules to guides that allow each partner to share themselves fully.

Temperature Reading provides a safe learning and sharing environment where each member of the couple can experiment with sharing his/her evolving self. It allows us to learn the skills to share ourselves whether we are feeling lovable or unlovable. Using Temperature Reading teaches us how to identify our feelings, how to acknowledge them and, most importantly, how to validate ourselves and each other when we are feeling and sharing them. This raises self-esteem and increases our ability to connect more deeply with our partner. Using this process with our partner enables us to transform our internal personal experiences into shared and intimate contact.

HOW TEMPERATURE READING WORKS

To develop and maintain intimacy couples need a time each day to reconnect with their partners. They also need a time and a place where they each talk about themselves, share their personal issues, and exchange essential information. Having a daily Temperature Reading allows couples to learn and practice these skills while enjoying the benefits of closer communication and acquiring an effective tool for increasing self esteem and intimacy.

A couple Temperature Reading is the daily practice of setting aside a time and place where a couple can check in with each other and share their appreciations, worries and concerns, puzzles, new information, hopes and wishes. Each of these is addressed in order. Each member of the couple takes a turn at being the sharer and the receiver in each category. Ten to fifteen minutes is recommended to cover each of the five categories. When issues, emotions or conflicts surface that will need more than the allotted time, they need to be identified (flagged) and then have a time set aside for their discussion after Temperature Reading. This provides a safety valve which allows the Temperature Reading to stay focused and continue moving on a positive note.

1. Appreciations

Sharing appreciations and excitements honors humanness. When a person shares an appreciation it results in good feelings for him/her and his/her partner. Appreciations are the giving of positive feedback and are an important source of positive and spontaneous energy. The sharing of appreciations creates authentic human connections between partners. This theme allows and encourages us to share our warm feelings of appreciation, excitement and specialness, no matter how small. Too often these are not shared. The sharing of appreciations allows each member of the couple the freedom to say what feels good to them, to speak for the things they like and to change their rules about sharing themselves and their good feelings.

2. Complaints with Recommendations, Worries, Concerns and Irritations

A complaint with a recommendation is the reporting of a discrepancy between what is and an idea or awareness of how things could be better. A person with a complaint is saying that the situation would be better "if." Allowing a person to share this information results in the person feeling validated. Most people have been taught not to complain or express worries and concerns because they would be criticizing someone. Including complaints, worries and concerns, and irritations gives permission for them to be thought about and provides a place for them to be shared, discussed and have solutions identified. It provides each member of the couple the freedom and opportunity to bring things up that they might otherwise shy away from disclosing. It helps the couple to speak about things they don't like or feel good about in a safe place. It is refreshing for people to learn that. Difficulties and discomforts can be listened to and addressed. Doing this in Temperature Reading enables the couple to focus the rest of their time and energy on more positive interactions.

Complaints and irritations left unexpressed often develop into negative interactions in relationships and restrict the openness that is required to maintain vitality, commitment, and elasticity in a relationship. Expressing irritations discharges negative feelings. The expression of worries and concerns allows each partner to express vulnerability, as well as fears and tensions that are present but not expressed. When partners voice them, fears and worries are better understood and their roots can be explored. Then they become less divisive in preventing intimacy.

3. Puzzles, Confusions, Questions, Rumors, Gossip

Every human relationship has some degree of puzzles, confusions, questions, gossip and rumors. These occur when an individual is needing to integrate some new information. Each is an opportunity to explore, clarify and to enhance the individual's and couple's understanding of situations and events to ensure that similar meaning is being made. Allowing, encouraging and acknowledging these questions in a clear and congruent way minimizes the distraction of peripheral feelings and thoughts and enables an individual who is struggling with an unnamed or unanswered question to free up their energy. Acknowledging that these areas exist and can be transformed through identifying and articulating them is unfamiliar to many people. Including this category allows each person the freedom to ask for what they need and allows them to share their feelings of uncertainty and confusion and to change their rules about not asking for help or identifying feelings.

4. New Information

New information is an important theme because people often have new information or announcements which need to be shared and discussed in order to be successfully integrated into a couple's daily life. Since people wonder about the best place to bring this information forward, this category provides a place where people can share their new information in a way that fits. Sharing new information routinely triggers recognition of additional items of importance that need to be shared. This keeps couples current and well-informed. Including this category allows each person the freedom to make choices about what information needs to be shared, allows them to share new things that have occurred and to change their rules about commenting.

5. Hopes and Wishes

Each person has within him/herself individual hopes, wishes and dreams that are unique to that person. This capacity to dream and visualize a tomorrow operates in every human being regardless of age. The purpose of this theme is to access individual and couple hopes and wishes so they can become more clearly heard. This is the first step in the process of actualizing them. The process of sharing these dreams in the couple relationship is important because, through sharing, each person learns of the other's hopes and wishes and can be in a better position to support his/her partner's efforts to obtain them. Including this category allows each person the freedom to dream, to hope, and to speak about what they yearn for. This begins to change their rules about asking for what they want and speaking about what they desire.

Flagging Items

There may be some appreciations, worries, complaints, puzzles or hopes and dreams that when shared need additional time to be discussed and resolved. When to pursue these sufficiently during Temperature Reading would distract from the process of moving from one theme to another, then these items need to be flagged. Flagging an item sets it aside temporarily so the Temperature Reading can continue, and the item can be addressed with the attention and involvement it requires. In these situations the specific item or issue can be noted and shared or explored more fully after the Temperature Reading is completed. An agreed upon block of time needs to be set aside after Temperature Reading for the resolution of flagged items. This process honors each item and provides a time and place for each to be adequately addressed.

DOING A TEMPERATURE READING

The couple needs to agree to set aside a specific length of time for the Temperature Reading, anywhere from 20-60 minutes. It is designed to be done daily or at least three times a week. The couple needs to agree to give their undivided attention to the process. This means no interruptions—no T.V., radio, or telephone. This also means no children until the couple is more familiar with doing Temperature Reading. Children can be included when the couple can stay focused on the process and are committed to staying on the task. Until then, if the couple has children, it may be best to do the Temperature Reading after the children have gone to bed.

The couple need to select a place to do Temperature Reading, a quiet corner somewhere in the home, outside or in any other private setting. The couple needs to be facing each other within a physical distance that feels safe to each. Generally this is about eighteen inches. Being at eye-level with good visibility is important since close physical proximity and being at eye-level facilitates the giving and receiving of all communication including the emotional aspects (Satir, 1988).

Temperature Reading starts by each member of the couple getting centered within themselves. This may be done many different ways. One way to become centered is to get in a comfortable position, close your eyes and get in touch with your own inner self and the inner self of your partner. Another is for both to become quiet, hold hands for a minute, to look at each other and embrace. After the centering, begin with the first theme.

Appreciations

Start with appreciations, excitements and surprises. You and your partner both go inside yourselves and find out what your own appreciations, excitements and surprises are. Appreciate what your partner has done by putting words to these acts or events. Share with your partner all the positives you have inside you that you have not communicated. Include them all no matter how trivial, corny or silly you may think they are. Make a mental note of what you want to share with your partner.

The following are areas couples can draw on for appreciations: specific things your partner has done, said or thought; anything your children, friends or relatives have done or said; and anything you have done, said or thought.

Centering. Close your eyes and go inside yourself and create a mental picture of each person in the room; check out if there is anything that you or your partner has done that you appreciate and haven't shared with him/her. Review today, yesterday, and the areas for appreciation.

Examples. I appreciate your setting the garbage cans out yesterday when I was in a hurry.

I appreciated your willingness to fix dinner for my family when you really didn't want to.

I appreciated your picking up the kids on such short notice.

How to give an appreciation. Use the person's name and say:

I liked it when you. . . .	It felt good when you. . . .
I was excited that you. . . .	I was surprised when you. . . .
I felt warm when you. . . .	I was glad that. . . .

How to respond to an appreciation. Identify the appreciation by making sure you hear accurately what your partner is telling you he or she appreciated. *Acknowledge the appreciation* by telling your partner the understanding you have of the appreciation he/she stated. *Validate the appreciation* by sharing how you can understand his or her point of view and how you appreciate them in their sharing it. *Integrate the appreciation* by thinking about how this sharing of appreciations benefits you both as a couple. *Transform an appreciation* by sharing with your partner how sharing these types of feelings and information can be of benefit to you as a couple.

Flag appreciations. When an appreciation brings up an issue that will take more time to discuss than is available during Temperature Reading, flag it. Do this by saying, "I think this area will take more time to address. Let's return to it after we finish." Write it down on your piece of paper and return to it when you finish Temperature Reading.

Complaints with Recommendations, Worries, Concerns and Irritations

Every relationship has complaints as well as elements of worry, concern and irritation. Identify what yours are and share them. The purpose of expressing them here is to bring them into the open and to hear the issues. This is the time for you to listen to the other person as if you were a detective listening to what the other person is concerned about. Listen to the person with the complaint and respond to that person.

It is best to do this by suspending judgment toward yourself and your partner. Look at this sharing of complaints as each person expressing their view of how the world could be a better place for them and for others. When understood this way, a complaint becomes a wish in disguise and not a statement that anyone has done anything wrong. This facilitates understanding of each other.

As the listener, after the complaint or irritation has been shared, validate that you've heard the complaint. Do this without becoming defensive or energized to act. Respond to the person with the complaint by stating your understanding of their concern. Look beyond the complaint, worry or concern for possible solutions by asking your partner what they see as solutions. An example of this is, "What do you suggest to improve the situation? Can you come up with three possibilities?"

The following are areas couples can draw on for complaints, worries and concerns, and irritations: others' acts, behavior, actions, words, unfulfilled promises, broken commitments, how one feels about an experience or situation or event in one's environment, the weather, their state of affairs.

Centering. Close your eyes and go inside yourself. Look, think, be aware of those things that have bothered you, that have left you unsettled, that you have had wishes for to be better, for those things that you had expectations, hopes and wishes for turning out differently, that you would have liked to be different, that left you disappointed, worried. Let yourself become aware of the new possibilities that would make these things better for you.

Example. Lori: I am angry because the house is a mess, and you committed yourself to clean yesterday and it's not done.

Bill: I hear you are angry because I committed myself to clean the house and it's not done yet (as I agreed to). I, too, get upset when somebody doesn't keep their commitment, and I was looking to having it done. I can understand your dissatisfaction.

How to Share a Complaint, Worry, Concern or Irritation

I didn't like it when you. . . .
I worry that. . . .
I am concerned about. . . .
I am afraid when/about/that. . . .
I was hurt when. . . .
I felt frustrated. . . .
I am uncomfortable with. . . .
_____ is too hot/cold.
_____ too much money/time.
_____ too long/short/far/near

Whenever a complaint is shared, be sure to accompany it with a recommendation for change. If one is not offered, the listener needs to ask the partner to share their recommendations or solutions.

How to respond to a complaint, worry, concern or irritation. *Identify* the complaint. *Acknowledge* the complaint—the person's experience—why they are sharing the complaint. *Validate* the person for sharing the complaint. *Integrate* the information from the sharing of the complaint. *Transform* the delivering of the complaint into an opportunity to discover new possibilities to make things better by using creative solutions.

Flagging complaints. When an issue is substantial enough to deserve more time than can be provided during Temperature Reading, it can be flagged by saying, "Let's flag it and put it as an agenda item to discuss after we finish." Write it down on your piece of paper and discuss it after Temperature Reading is over.

Puzzles, Confusions, Questions, Rumors and Gossip

Third comes the theme of Puzzles, Confusions, Questions, Rumors and Gossip, which allows partners to keep this area of their relationship up-to-date and current. Partners are encouraged to share vague and peripheral thoughts and feelings. This is the place where gossip or third party information is addressed and clarified. Often in relationships we have puzzles or questions in our mind that when expressed help us learn more about what we don't know. This also allows our partner to be informed and to share in our puzzlement. By clarifying and sharing our puzzles, confusions, rumors and gossip, we are enhancing our own and our mate's understanding of situations and events. This leads to similar meaning being made and shared. The following are areas couples can draw on for Puzzles, Confusions, Questions, Rumors and Gossip: behavior, feelings or information.

Centering. Take a minute to go inside yourself. Is there anything I have a question about or am puzzled with that pertains to this relationship? Am I confused about anything? Is there anything I need to know from my partner? Have I heard any rumors or gossip about me, my partner, our relationship or loved ones that I need to check out? Let yourself become aware of any questions you have or information you need or would like.

Examples. Mary: I am puzzled about how we can take the car in for repairs, go to the store, and pick up Aunt Martha all on the same day; I'm perplexed.

Mary: I am puzzled why you *always* have to be the last one to bed.

Larry: I am confused, Jane. You are always eager to have company over, yet you become so upset just before they arrive — cleaning and tidying up — that you seem to be uptight when they get here; it ruins some of my fun in having company over.

Larry: I heard a comment by one of my friends that your brother and his wife are not getting along.

How to Share a Puzzle, Confusion,
Question, Rumor or Gossip

I am puzzled about. . . .
I am trying to figure out. . . .
I am trying to make sense out of. . . .
I became confused when you *did*, said. . . .
I have a question about. . . .
I heard _____ and want to check it out with you.
I heard the following rumor _____.
I heard talk that _____.
There is gossip going around that _____.

How to respond to the sharing of a puzzle, confusion, question, rumor or gossip. Identify the puzzle by stating your understanding of the puzzle: "I hear that you are puzzled about. . . . Is this an accurate statement about your puzzle? If not, please correct me." Work at this until both partners agree on the puzzle. At times this may be the most important piece of work to complete. It produces understanding.

Acknowledge their puzzle. "I can *see, understand, sense, feel, think* that you are puzzled by _____." *Validate* the person's sharing their puzzle with you. "While I get frustrated by your puzzles, I appreciate your bringing them up so we can resolve them, or at least be aware of them."

Integrate the meaning of the sharing of the puzzle. "By talking about our puzzles, I become more aware of the less obvious things you are mulling over. When you share your puzzles, confusions, questions, rumors and gossip, it gives me a chance to share what you and I feel, sense, and to come closer to you."

Flagging a Puzzle. When one of the items in this theme appears to "trigger" other feelings, or it appears a specific item will take more than a few minutes, "flag it." This is done by identifying the issue as being worthy of more time and focus. "I think this will take more time, let's flag it and set it aside." Then write it down on your piece of paper and return to it when you finish Temperature Reading.

New Information

This is the place to share new information, changed information and announcements. Put into words any event, announcement or news that has transpired or changed since the couple was last together.

Areas from which couples can draw new information and announcements are: work, friends, telephone calls, personal contacts, reading, TV, radio, neighbors, mail, children, relatives and personal life data.

Centering. Take a few seconds to be quiet and see what New Information you have. This can be written down on a list. Select what you want to share from your list. It is not necessary to share everything on it.

Example. Liza: My mother is very ill, and I want to go visit her for the weekend.

Tom: I hear that your mother is ill, and you are finding it important to spend the weekend with her.

Liza: Yes. We need to do something about our previous plans.

Tom: Yes. I am disappointed; I was looking forward to our spending the weekend planting our garden.

Liza: Is there anything I can do or get for you before I leave? I was thinking of leaving Friday night and returning Sunday about 5:30 p.m. How is this for you? You know you are welcome to come with me.

The *identifying* and *acknowledgement* of New Information is completed when the person shares the information, and the other person acknowledges the receiving it.

Flagging New Information. When New Information will take extended time, it can be flagged by saying, "This New Information will take a lot of time to address. Let's return to it at the completion of New Information." Write it down on your sheet of flagged items to be addressed.

Hopes and Wishes

Hopes and wishes are longings and yearnings one has for the future. When they are expressed, they have a better chance of being realized, and your partner can connect with your positive energy. In order to get in touch with your hopes and wishes, be sure to get agreement that you are both ready to go into this theme. Decide who will share his/her hopes and wishes first. This can be done by taking turns, with each person sharing one hope or wish, or having one partner do his/her entire list and then the other.

Areas from which couples can draw hopes and wishes are: present behavior, feelings, thoughts, the future, what one hopes for in relationships with others or personally.

Centering. Each of you take 30 seconds, close your eyes and ask yourself: What do I hope for myself? What are my personal dreams and wishes? What hopes, wishes and dreams do I have for our relationship? Open your eyes. You might want to write your answers down before you start. This frees you up to hear your partner's hopes and wishes and serves as a reminder of your selection to share.

Examples. I would really like to stop smoking. As part of my self-improvement program, I hope to start an exercise program. I hope we are able to spend a few days alone together within the next few weeks. I have the dream of becoming a Little League coach. I am really hoping my negative feelings toward _____ go away, and I can be more accepting. I think it would be great if our next family vacation could be one where we all went camping.

When you are hearing your partner's Hopes and Wishes, it becomes increasingly more effective when you report back, "I hear you are hoping to take up an exercise program. What do you need to start, and when will you begin? I think it is exciting if you start exercising."

Example: Tina: I hope we can plan a vacation that enriches each of us and our relationship.

John: I hear you hope we can have a vacation that brings us closer together.

Tina: Yes.

John: I am surprised, because I thought you were pleased with the way we have handled vacations, and I was worried there wouldn't be time for us. But I am glad you brought it up.

Tina: Let's flag this and talk more after the Temperature Reading about our Hopes and Wishes for our vacations.

John: Sounds like a good idea, because I have some other hopes and wishes I wanted to share before we finish.

Closing the Temperature Reading

After completing the Temperature Reading, take a minute to discuss how it could be improved. You might share how you thought and felt about doing it. Set a time for the next one. Choose one person to be in charge of getting the Temperature Reading started.

Now look at your partner. Close your eyes. Go inside and become aware of how you feel about yourself and your partner now. What would you like to say? to do? to enhance or present yourself next time? Let yourself be aware of these things. Then open your eyes and make a commitment to your partner for the next Temperature Reading. Set a specific date, time and place for your next temperature reading. A specific time is very important and at times may have to be negotiated.

Flagged Items

Now is the time to look at your list of flagged items. If there are one or more items, you and your partner need to review the list and see how much time you'll need to spend on each issue. Then you'll need to contract for that amount of time either now, or set aside a time to do that. For example, "There are two items we need to address. Let's set a time and place to do that." If there are no flagged items, then you are finished. In a way that fits for you, bring this to a close, i.e., shake hands, hug, kiss, etc.

OTHER THERAPEUTIC APPLICATIONS USING TEMPERATURE READING

Temperature Reading can be utilized as described in this article in the therapy session itself, allowing the therapist a format for assessing and facilitating effective communication between the couple. It can also be used when working in therapy when only one partner is engaged in therapy. Another application is to use it with a couple in therapy. In addition, it can be used with individuals, couples and groups in Meditations (Zahnd, in press).

In working therapeutically with one partner, an individual Temperature Reading can be applied in two different ways. One is to guide the person through the themes of Temperature Reading focusing on him/herself. For example: "John, what do you appreciate about yourself?" Wait for the answer or tell what you appreciate. "What are you excited about? Do you have any surprises today? What are your complaints about yourself today? What are you confused about? Do you have any puzzles, confusions, rumors or gossip? Do you have any new information you want to share about yourself? What are your Hopes, Wishes and Dreams for yourself?"

In doing Temperature Reading with John as one part of the couple, the process might go like this: "John, when you think about Lucy, your partner, what do you appreciate about her? Let's make a *list*! Which ones have you shared, wanted to share? What prevents you? How would this be different if she heard these?"

"O.K., John, let's go on. When you think about Lucy, what are your complaints about her and your relationship? Let's make a list. What keeps these from being shared? What are possible solutions to the complaints? Could you share these with her?"

This could be assigned as homework with the individual or couple. It can be followed up in the next therapy session.

Temperature Reading has been used in Meditations with couples and groups (Zahnd, in press). A meditation with couples might go something like this:

> I want each of you to get comfortable in your chairs, close your eyes and go inside, creating a picture of yourself with your partner. If you have this picture, raise your hand. Now, place yourself and your partner in a safe and nurturing context facing each other. As you look at your partner, what do you appreciate about him/her? Picture yourself telling him/her. How is this for you, for the other person? What are your complaints?" Go through each theme of Temperature Reading. At

the end, ask each partner what s/he would like to share with his/her partner; ask them to tell you what it was like for each of them.

CLOSING

Temperature Reading is a powerful and effective tool for use in the therapeutic process with couples. It is also an asset in helping each member of the couple surface his/her own truths with support and nurturing by opening closed communication patterns and increasing the possibility of intimacy. When an individual maintains a closed or restricted communication system, energy is expended to maintain defenses. This dissipates the allocation of energy for survival. The higher amount of energy expended to maintain and manage internal components diminishes the amount of energy available for moving forward in the social world for meeting needs or pursuing dreams.

Each individual comes to the couple relationship with experience operating from a personal framework of openness or closedness. This has been developed from their experiences in their family of origin and previous efforts at coupling (Stone & Winkelman, 1989). Their willingness and skill in sharing themselves with each other will influence how they communicate about their interpersonal relationship and other issues. Each person in the relationship has a range of openness for communication and activates their range of openness and closedness differently. Different issues can activate or trigger the person to move toward a closed or open system. Therefore each person's communication range can be expanded or restricted depending on whether the couple has created an open or closed communication system. The use of the Temperature Reading's safe and structured format increases the range of openness in a couple's communication system. Using the Temperature Reading process teaches the couple how to move from a restricted communication system to an open communication system.

The first step to effective and healthy long-term coupling is a deep acceptance of our own internal process of feeling and responding. Once each individual becomes aware of the possibility of sharing and learning about each other's unique inside self, communication is enhanced and leads to deeper intimacy, love and contentedness. The Temperature Reading process is one of the vehicles that has been found to be beneficial in assisting in the process of each person opening his/her internal processes to self-exploration and to the intimate sharing exploration that is so vital in all healthy and functional coupling.

REFERENCES

Bandler, R., Grinder, J., & Satir, V. (1976). *Changing with families*. Palo Alto, CA: Science and Behavior Books.

Banmen, J., & Gerber, J. (Eds.). (1985). *Virginia Satir's meditations and inspirations*. Berkeley, CA: Celestial Art.

Beck, A.T. (1988). *Love is never enough*. New York, NY: Harper & Row Publishers.

Dinkmeyer, D., & Carlson, J. (1986, Spring). Time for a better marriage. *Journal of Psychotherapy and the Family*, *2*(1), 19-28.

Gottman, J.M. (1982, Summer). Emotional responsiveness in marital conversations. *Journal of Communication*, *32*(3), 108-120.

Napier, A. Y. (1988). *The fragile bond*. New York, NY: Harper & Row Publishers.

Satir, V. (1982). (1967). (1964). *Conjoint family therapy*. Palo Alto, CA: Science and Behavior Books.

Satir, V. (1972). *Peoplemaking*. Palo Alto, CA: Science and Behavior Books.

Satir, V. (1975). *Self-esteem*. Millbrae, CA: Celestial Arts.

Satir, V. (1976). *Making contact*. Millbrae, CA: Celestial Arts.

Satir, V. (1978). *Your many faces*. Millbrae, CA: Celestial Arts.

Satir, V., Stachowiak, J., & Taschman, H. (1977). *Helping families to change*. New York: Aronson.

Satir, V., & Baldwin, M. (1983). *Satir step by step*. Palo Alto, CA: Science and Behavior Books.

Satir, V. (1988). *The new peoplemaking*. Mountain View, CA: Science and Behavior Books, Inc.

Schwab, J., Baldwin, M., Gerber, J., Gomori, M., & Satir, V. (1989). *The Satir approach to communication* (A workshop manual). Palo Alto, CA: Science and Behavior Books.

Solomon, M.F. (1989). *Narcissism and intimacy: Love and marriage in an age of confusion*. New York: W.W. Norton & Co., Inc.

Stone, H., & Winkelman, S. (1989). *Embracing each other: Relationship as teacher, healer & guide*. San Rafael, CA: New World Library.

Stone, H., & Winkelman, S. (1990). The vulnerable child. In J. Abrams (Ed.),

Reclaiming the inner child (pp. 176-184). Los Angeles, CA: Jeremy P. Tarcher, Inc.

Thomas, S.P., Albrecht, K., & White, P. (1984, October). Determinants of marital quality in dual career couples. *Family Relations Journal of Applied Family and Child Studies, 33*(4), 513-521.

Tuites, A.H., & Tuites, D.E. (1986, June). Equality in male/female relationships. *Individual Psychology Journal of Adlerian Theory, Research and Practice, 42*(2), 191-200.

Wampler, K.S. (1982, July). The effectiveness of the Minnesota couple communication program: A review of research. *Journal of Marital and Family Therapy, 8*(3), 345-355.

Welwood, J. (Ed.). (1985). *Challenge of the heart: Love, sex, and intimacy in changing times.* Boston: Shambhala Publications, Inc.

Zahnd, W.F. (1987). *Crested Butte temperature reading chart.* Paradise, CA: Author.

Zahnd, W.F. (in press). Temperature reading. In J. Banmen & J. Weinberg (Eds.), *Satir in action.*

Zimmer, D. (1983, Winter). Interaction patterns and communication skills in sexually distressed, maritally distressed, and normal couples: Two experimental studies. *Journal of Sex and Marital Therapy, 9*(4), 251-265.

Family Reconstruction:
The Masterpiece of Virginia Satir

William Nerin

SUMMARY. The author claims that a process developed by Virginia Satir and called "Family Reconstruction" by her, is the epitome of her contribution to the field of therapy. This article describes the process, its goals and theory, the conditions necessary for an effective therapeutic breakthrough. How this therapeutic process can be powerfully effective in healing couple's relationships is shown. In a final note, Nerin suggests that Satir's model not be dubbed "communication theory," but called "eco-psychological."

It is an honor to write this article in this issue dedicated to Virginia Satir. It is a small measure of gratitude to her for giving the world family reconstruction.

Family reconstruction was developed by Virginia Satir in the late 1960's. I believe this process is the epitome of her creative genius. The more I guide family reconstructions the more I see that Virginia's body of thought, methods and approaches are expressed in this growth process. Family reconstruction is a blend of psychodrama,

William Nerin, MA, MFT, is a family therapist and a long time student, friend and colleague of the late Virginia Satir, a pioneer in the field of family therapy. He is the author of *Family Reconstruction, Long Day's Journey Into Light*, W.W. Norton, NY 1986; Adjunct Assistant Professor of Human Relations at the University of Oklahoma; the co-founder with his wife Anne Robertson-Nerin, PhD, of the Family Reconstruction Training Institute. He travels extensively, teaching and consulting throughout the world, especially in the field of family of origin work and self esteem. He received his MA from Columbia University-Teacher's College, NY 1965. He has lived most of his adult life in Oklahoma and has recently moved to Gig Harbor, WA on an acreage in the midst of trees where he enjoys the peaceful rhythms of nature. Correspondence may be sent to 11221 35th Ave Ct. N.W., Gig Harbor, WA 98335.

gestalt, sculpting, altered states of consciousness and fantasy—
within the framework of family systems theory and nurturing love.
Since family reconstruction embodies Virginia's thought and approach to the human being, participating in family reconstruction is
participating in Virginia's spirit and philosophy.

I will give a brief description of a family reconstruction and then
outline the goals of the process and the theory behind it. I will later
illustrate how family reconstruction facilitated an explorer to become part of a couple. I will conclude with further thoughts about
Virginia's contribution to the field of therapy.

Family Reconstruction takes place with a group of some 10 to 20
people. The person doing her or his reconstruction whom I call the
Explorer (Virginia calls the Star) chooses members of the group to
play the roles of members of his or her families, the family of origin, maternal and paternal families. The Explorer's current family
is not dealt with directly. The theory is that the Explorer's current
dilemmas, problems, growth potentials often are powerfully connected to the way he or she was raised. So at times the most effective way to help a person is to deal with those early learnings and
experiences by going back to where those experiences took place.
The idea is not to relive them; it is to experience them in a new way.

Family reconstruction is led by a trained guide. In this chapter I
shall call the Explorer, Joe. The guide usually asks Joe to pick
someone to play his part during the day. This stand-in I refer to as
the alter ego. Then Joe picks his mother and father. Those three
most important people, the mother, father and alter ego will be
enrolled and remain enrolled for the entire reconstruction. The
guide then decides which family to develop first, the maternal or
paternal family. For illustration, let's say the guide chooses to do
the material family first. The guide asks Joe to choose members
from the group to play the roles of the members of the maternal
family, the family his mother grew up in.

There are three basic ways to enroll the role players. One, the
Explorer is invited to speak directly to the role players, e.g., Joe
says, "Helen (the maternal grandmother), you were born in 1860 in
Rome, New York. You are the oldest of 11 children. Your father is
a successful lawyer. The family was well provided for. When you
are 18 you meet Jonathan Breenly whom you marry when you are

19 years old. You have artistic abilities and your paintings win awards. You will have your first child in 1882 when you are 22 years old. When you are 25, you and your husband and child will move to New York City and you will live there the rest of your life. You will have six children and you will be well known for your art work."

The second and most powerful way to enroll is to have the Explorer place the role player in a physical position as if to make a sculpt of the person that best represents the way the person appears to the Explorer. As guide, I often tell the Explorer, "Joe, I want you to put Pete (the role player) in a physical position as if you were a famous sculptor. Consider Pete a block of marble and you are going to make a sculpture of him to be put into a museum so that viewers will be able to say 'ah, this is the kind of person Joe's father is.'" At times I'll ask the Explorer to sculpt the person alone, at other times with his wife, and at other times within the entire family.

In the process I ask the Explorer to examine every detail; the tilt of the head, position of hands and fingers, legs, the entire posture until the Explorer is finally satisfied with the sculpt. Then I tell the sculpted person to remain frozen and "let yourself be aware of the series of feelings and thoughts that arise in you." I hold the sculpted person in the position for what seems a long time to the others in the room since it takes some time for the role player to get in touch with all the feelings that the sculpted position generates.

It is amazing to the Explorer how true to life are the feelings and thoughts the role players express from being in the sculpt. So often Explorers say, "Wow, that's really on target," "Dad was just that way," "Mother used to say exactly what you just said."

So powerful is this technique that it moves the Explorer to accept as valid what later unfolds in the psychodrama as new pictures and insights.

The third way the role players get more into their role is through the psychodrama the role players will be enacting. For example, I'll ask Joe to sculpt his father's parents as he envisions they were at the time of their marriage in 1885. As they are positioned in that sculpt I'll then ask the first child to be born by crawling between the legs of the mother. I direct the baby, mother and father to move non verbally to any position their feelings and thoughts dictate to them. After they reposition themselves at the birth of their first offspring, I'll freeze them again for a minute or so, inviting them to be aware of their feelings and thoughts. Then I invite the three to share their feelings and thoughts.

Next I'll bring the second and remaining children into the family and repeat the directions. As each child is born, different positions are taken and different feelings and thoughts arise. I will repeat the process for other significant events in the family such as moves, sicknesses, deaths, the depression of the 1930's, being expelled from school, bouts with alcoholism. As Joe sees and hears all this, he appreciates what the circumstances were at his father's birth and how those influenced the way his father was raised and felt about himself.

There are a variety of ways the psychodramas are directed to take place. For example, the birth of the Explorer may be a very detailed and elaborate scene involving doctor, nurses, waiting room, delivery room with the mother getting into the spirit of the scene with words and/or grimaces.

These are the ways the role players move progressively into the skins of the family members. The first two, directly speaking to the role player and sculpting are so powerful, that the person is usually sufficiently enrolled so that the ensuing psychodrama becomes authentically real to the Explorer.

The work done with the paternal and maternal families is to achieve two goals. One goal is to enroll the mother and father of the Explorer so that they will be able to create with some authenticity the family that the Explorer was raised in. The second goal is to allow the Explorer to have a full psychological experience of appreciating how his or her mother and father became the kind of persons they were emanating from their respective families. I deliberately choose the words "full psychological experience." The Explorer in a family reconstruction hopefully gains more than intellectual insight. Joe is moved by the sculpting and psychodrama on all levels, intellectual, emotional and physical. With this day's appreciations, the door is opened for Joe to see his parents as humans rather than as parents. When this happens, Joe can give a full "yes" to those two persons as being part him. Thus he is alive with his roots! This is critical because so often we build a wall between ourselves and our *parent's* behavior to protect ourselves. This wall can be a wall of anger, a wall of denial or withdrawal, or a wall of submission. It is the behavior of people in their roles as parents that can bother us. We need to go beyond the "parental" behavior to the deeper human being behind the role of parent.

It is important to note however, that while giving full acceptance to one's roots is one of the ultimate goals of family reconstruction, an intermediate goal is sometimes achieved. That goal is to allow the Explorer to discover anger and walls, grief and sadness, that have been buried for years. If these walls are uncovered then the Explorer will need time to deal with the newfound anger and other barriers that may arise. So at the end of the day's reconstruction, the Explorer may need to distance oneself from a mother or father. But now the barrier or anger is surfaced so that the Explorer can deal with it in the days ahead. This intermediate goal of surfacing what was hidden will open the way eventually for the Explorer to accept his or her roots.

In sculpting and psychodrama scenes, the Explorer sees things he or she never thought of before. Empty holes are filled explaining why and how the parents are the way they are. Joe experiences the kind of self-esteem his parents possessed, how fragile or strong the self worth is and what threatens his parents. As a result of these experiences Joe begins to understand and feel compassion for his parents, or as mentioned above the need to be distant from them for a while.

After doing both the maternal and paternal families, Joe's own family of origin is reconstructed. At this point I want to emphasize two very important points I have learned over the years in doing family reconstructions.

First, it is *more important* to reconstruct the maternal and paternal families than to do the family of origin! Many Explorers want to launch right into their family origin, skipping the maternal and paternal families, because they feel that there is where the meat of the matter is. In a sense they are correct, for it is in that family that they derived the dysfunctional patterns that are still afflicting them in their present lives. However the paradox is that relief from those dysfunctional patterns will occur more out of doing the maternal and paternal families than in the family of origin.

The reason for this is profound. Early childhood impressions and learnings are so powerful because the child is so vulnerable and the parents are like gods. By seeing one's mother and father being raised in their families, the Explorer senses in a very profound way that these two "gods" are indeed human. As the Explorer sees how his or her father was a baby himself, went through the same journey basically as every child, then on a deep unconscious level the Explorer affirms – he is just like me. The "god-like" hold is broken. I will have more to say about this later on.

The second reason why treating the maternal and paternal families is more important than treating the family of origin is that the Explorer already has some knowledge of the family of origin, even though immaturely grasped and interpreted. The Explorer has lived in that family and has *only* experienced mother and father as the adults they were at the time and thereafter the birth of the Explorer. The Explorer has never experienced the parents as babies, growing youngsters, teenagers, and young adults. The Explorer has never experienced the budding sexuality of the parents, their vulnerable condition as children. Giving the Explorer the chance to experience this part of their parents lives supplies the Explorer with much new information and realization that they are humans.

So if there is time and energy to do Joe's family of origin I do it. In doing this, Joe sees his mother and father first meet each other. He sees scenes leading to the engagement and marriage. He sees their shyness, bravado, confidence, awkwardness, sexuality, fears, fun, flirtations. Joe witnesses their marriage, the birth of his siblings and his own birth. He captures the emotions of each family member. He understands the strengths and weaknesses of each family member and how those strengths and weaknesses interact.

Throughout the unfolding of these three families there will be times when Joe is emotionally moved. At such moments Joe might be invited to have a more direct interaction with a family member. For example, when tears enter Joe's eyes at the death of his sister, he is asked to step forward to share his feelings and thoughts with her. Perhaps unfinished grief is brought to closure in this scene.

In a scene that Joe begins to feel anger toward his mother he is invited to express himself to her which may be the first time Joe has allowed himself to be angry with her. If Joe has a problem in having fun, when he sees his brother horsing around in a scene, Joe is invited to exchange places with his brother and continue the scene. As Joe is playful he may be breaking a family rule, of "always be responsible." Thus playing such a scene, he begins to be freer.

When Joe is not moved by a scene where emotions would normally arise, he might be invited to be a member in the scene so that his feelings could be stimulated. If that may be too threatening for Joe, his Alter Ego could be moved in and then Joe could see the reaction in his Alter Ego. This might enable Joe to break through a barrier that had been in him for years.

So throughout the family reconstruction every opportunity is taken to allow the Explorer to have new experiences, new understandings, new feelings, new behavior. In this way dysfunctional rules and meanings can be broken, suppressed feelings can be released, fears can be walked through, behavior understood so hard feelings can be softened, unfinished business finished. In this way anger, hatred and bitterness can be transformed into understanding, compassion and forgiveness; walls of separation can be dissolved with tenderness and closeness resulting.

The fact that the Explorer has such a full and powerful psychological experience is due to the fact that live people, authentically enrolled, acting out scenes that once occurred in the family history stimulate the eyes, ears, skin, memory, feelings, mind, imagination of the Explorer in a way no mere talking about such data can. This is why in family reconstruction the Explorer can be moved profoundly so that deep structural changes take place on an emotional level.

An effective reconstruction is one in which several elements are present. One is that the Explorer is ripe for the family reconstruction; i.e., he or she has powerful motivation to be open and to change, and has arrived at a special moment in life for the next step of development. Two, the group is made up of people who genuinely care for the Explorer so that the room is filled with the energy of love, for growth can occur only in the warmth of love. Third, the guide not only is caring but also is competent in the task of guiding the reconstruction, communicating well with the Explorer and during the process continually inviting the Explorer to be decisive over his or her destiny in the new unfolding of the Explorer's life. As all this begins to be felt by the Explorer, the Explorer is willing to trust on the deepest level.

When all these factors coalesce then all that is possible to be achieved on that given day will be accomplished. Total growth will not be met, but that growth appropriate to the stage of development the Explorer is in will be met.

What are the goals to be achieved in a family reconstruction? I list here two sets of goals, the first lists the goals of the family reconstruction itself; the second lists the operating goals of the guide.

GOALS OF FAMILY RECONSTRUCTION

1. To gain new insights and pictures of one's maternal, paternal family and family of origin. These new perceptions lead to different feelings about family members and *consequently about oneself*.

2. To enable the Explorer to experience mother and father as human as the Explorer experiences him/herself, rather than in their roles, as parents, grandparents, etc. Meeting parents on the common ground of one's humanity invisibly tends to break the powerful bindings of the godlike given rules, meanings, ways of relating and coping, received as children from these all powerful parents.

3. To complete unfinished business—e.g., to release suppressed feelings and meanings such as to grieve over some loss, to discover hidden anger, to face the pain of one's childhood rather than deny it.

4. To let the Explorer discover if he or she has a deep, pervasive and hidden need to change one's parents (e.g., to get them to be approving or accepting of the Explorer. If this is going on then the Explorer can be helped to see that the need is to change self, not parent. This helps the Explorer see the need to get acceptance from self rather than from others. While it is normal to want acceptance from one's parents, to still need it as an adult on a survival level is not beneficial to one's self esteem.

5. To allow the Explorer to bond with the family roots in this *new, adult, human* way. This bonding occurs because the Explorer

now has understanding, empathy and compassion with the family members as individual human beings. When this reconnecting happens the Explorer *says yes* to her or his roots! When this is done the Explorer completes self. By saying yes to one's root system, rather than denying or opposing, increases *self esteem*. To achieve increased positive self esteem *is the most important and over arching goal of a family reconstruction*. This involves a dramatic shift in one's self identity.

GOALS IN GUIDING

1. To do all that is within one's imagination and creativity to allow the Explorer to make a true *human* connection with the family members. Besides the enrollment processes as sculpting and psychodrama, other techniques are used, for example, having the Explorer speak directly to a family member; let the Explorer step into a sculpture of one of the members; activate the fantasy and imagination of the Explorer by speaking as a family member, e.g., the mother or grandfather; let the Explorer be free to touch family members; to insert the Explorer in the drama of certain scenes so that the Explorer can relive these scenes in a new way, e.g., to substitute the Explorer in the place of the alter ego that allows the Explorer to grasp the subtleties of the transaction and dynamics that as a youngster he or she could not understand. This new understanding helps the Explorer perceive and feel family members in a new way, which adds to the Explorer.

2. To fill in missing parts, e.g., constructing scenes where fun and laughter occurred when the Explorer can't imagine this ever happening in the family; letting the Explorer see some limitations in the parent held as angel and some strengths in the parent held as devil; constructing the biological parents of a adopted Explorer.

3. To nurture and honor the arousal of emotions that well up in the Explorer.

4. To empower the Explorer. This happens in many different ways from respecting what the Explorer wants to achieve on the day itself, to allowing the Explorer to feel and express herself or himself as the day progresses. The Explorer of course is empowered from

the overall process of being filled up with new understandings, feelings and in reconnecting in a new way with his or her roots.

I have briefly described a family reconstruction and its goals. Now I turn to the rationale behind it. I want to illustrate the rationale by sharing with you a true story, disguised to protect the identities of those in the story.

A little girl was born into a family and soon discovered that she had a father, mother and brother. Things went easy for the baby girl. Her every need was addressed. When hungry she was satisfied, when soiled, she was cleaned. Most of all she was held close to her mother's bosom and felt her warmth and love. Soon the baby discovered she had a name, Elizabeth. Early on Elizabeth heard laughter and all kinds of pleasant sounds. On some deep level Elizabeth knew all was well. Later on she learned the language that described her state of being — she felt loved and wanted. In some enchanted way she knew she was special.

To these initial impressions other impressions were later added. When Elizabeth was about a year and a half old her father lost his job in the depression of the early '30's. He fell into despair, became listless and soon was called lazy by his wife, Diane. Frank, the father and Diane, the mother, fought a lot. The earlier pleasant sounds turned to harsh, ugly, scary, angry sounds. It sounded as if Elizabeth's world was going out of control. The little girl became frightened.

Diane got a job as a seamstress while Frank moved from one job to another never supporting the family "as he should" — as Elizabeth heard from her mother's lips. It was clear to three-year-old Elizabeth that Mother was right and Dad was wrong. Mother suffered much and Dad caused it. Besides Dad was gone a lot and never played with Elizabeth.

Meanwhile, Elizabeth's older brother, Dennis became restless. About two years after Elizabeth's birth, he became jealous of her as she was such an easy baby compared to him. Dennis began to think there was something wrong with him. Being a super sensitive kid, Dennis was deeply hurt when he heard the arguing, blaming and fighting between Mother and Dad. Dennis tried to make some sense of all this and concluded that it was his fault that everything was wrong in the family. Being the first born he was raised to be very responsible so he took on the responsibility of what was going on. Why Dennis even heard his Mother say "how are we going to feed the kids?" Dennis concluded that if he weren't around the family wouldn't be so poor and bad off. As the pain in the family intensified Dennis began to scream out for the cessation of the pain and fighting. He did this by becoming more and more delinquent. He got into trouble at school and later in his teens he began to drink, fight and got thrown in jail.

While all this was going on, Elizabeth also made a strange conclusion. She decided that she had to make her Mother happy since her Mother was not getting her happiness from Frank and Dennis. The way to do this is to please her by being perfectly obedient. The more Elizabeth became obedient, the more Dennis grew jealous and hurt and cried out all the more through his delinquency. Diane threw up her hands and grew closer to her obedient and loving daughter for happiness and peace. Diane also became more self sufficient through her work in the world.

Elizabeth, being so close to her mother, felt Diane's fear of making ends meet since Frank was "going down hill." Elizabeth became like her Mother. She feared that she wouldn't survive and coped by becoming self-sufficient and independent as Diane was becoming. Little Elizabeth was learning a rather complex way to be in the world. She is to please others in order to make them happy, while at the same time be independent so as to survive. Elizabeth was also learning to use others if you have to in order to be happy, since she was being inappropriately used by Diane for this purpose. Life was becoming confusing and painful for Elizabeth given this set of circumstances.

Both Dennis and Elizabeth found reasons to leave home early after graduating from high school.

Elizabeth was 39 and single. She had become a leading feminist attorney in Chicago, bright, shrewd, attractive, personable and very independent. Her charming personality charged with enormous capacities to be pleasing while at the same time independent and inaccessible made her the challenge of scores of equally bright and attractive men. She enjoyed them all but never seemed to find that one true love of life.

When Elizabeth was 40 she encountered a powerful and lovingly accepting female therapist who invited her to a family reconstruction group in which she did her own family reconstruction. Fourteen months after her reconstruction she married a most wonderful man.

Now to the rationale of these dynamics and of family reconstruction.

Elizabeth came into the world totally dependent on her parents for her physical, emotional and psychological survival. She was like a blank blackboard in the sense that her genetic package contained no set of instruction as to how to relate to others, what are the meanings of life's events, who and what kind of a person she is, what are the rules of living and how does one cope when threatened in life.

As the story shows, Elizabeth learned to relate to others by pleasing them, how to cope with threats to survival by being independent and successful in the world. Her childhood experiences taught her not to depend on men — learning a meaning about men from Mother's fear that men cannot be trusted. The way Elizabeth was related to, told her what kind of a person she was. In our story she learned at first that she was a very special person, beloved by her parents. She was indeed worth much. Then she learned that she was a person to make others happy as she strove to make her Mother happy. At first, Elizabeth viewed her parents as gods, all powerful, all knowing, perfect. Later, the "god" was only her Mother. What truths Elizabeth learned from her parents especially her Mother carried the weight of divine authority. The teachings on Elizabeth's blackboard were written in blood as it were. One thing Elizabeth learned for sure was that she must not displease her parents too much else she would not survive. If both parents became angry at her, they might abandon her (another conclusion drawn by the immature mind of a child).

Add to all this is the fact that Elizabeth's mind as a little girl is not fully developed. So Elizabeth tends to see things in simplistic blacks and whites. She is capable of making strange, unreal conclusions. For example, Elizabeth decided it was up to her to make her Mother happy; and that her Dad was bad. Dennis decided that he was not as good as Elizabeth; that he was to blame for the family problems. Elizabeth feared surviving, even though in reality she was very secure.

Add to this a third factor. Connected to one's perceptions is a powerful set of emotions. Elizabeth felt the warmth and closeness of love, the fear of surviving, the guilt of disobedience, the hurt and fear at seeing Dad the devil, the confusion in trying to be self sufficient and pleasing to others, the shame in using people.

So it is with all humans. Each growing child learns a way of seeing things, a set of meanings about the events. Each person forms feelings around those perceptions. The most important learnings are (1) how to relate and be related to; (2) the meanings of self and life; (3) the rules to live by; (4) how to cope with threats. These truths, embedded in feelings, are deeply entrenched in the growing child.

Most of these learnings are functional, i.e., growth producing; some are not. Many are appropriate for one stage of life and inappropriate at another stage of life.

As these myriad experiences of life are taken in by Elizabeth they build inside of her and combine in a variety of ways to add up to two most fundamental impressions; what kind of person I am and how worthwhile I am. These two impressions are one's self identity and self esteem.

Since these critical perceptions and conclusions are made by an immature mind, they can often be distorted and therefore inaccurate. Since these early learnings are often dysfunctional and deeply etched in the personality, a powerful experience is needed to transform them into functional learnings. This is where family reconstruction comes in.

The Explorer is a grown person who is now capable of understanding the data: the missing facts, the complicated and subtle psychological traits and reality of parents and siblings, the dynamics and transactions of certain important family events that went on when that person was a child. So if the grown person has a chance to relive in the safe environment of a family reconstruction those early moments of life he or she can relive them in a new way. The *adult* can get more accurate understandings of those early experiences. As the perceptions of mother, father, brothers, sisters, self, events shift so do the emotions attached to these perceptions. As these perceptions and feelings shift then the embedded set of learnings about relating, meanings, rules and survival mechanisms also shift. As these shift so do one's personal identity and self worth.

Take our story of Elizabeth. Her family reconstruction done at the age of 40 very likely allowed her to see how her father, Frank, came to the marriage with Diane with a view of himself as the responsible wage earner. His entire self identity and self esteem revolved around his being a man who supports his family. Through the family reconstruction Elizabeth saw for the first time the enormous impact Frank's father's early death had on Frank. Frank as a teenager went to work and successfully supported the family for which he was deeply loved and appreciated — as was his father while alive. So Elizabeth could appreciate now for the first time what a crushing blow it was to Frank's self worth not to support his family during the depression of the '30's. The depression led many to suicide, it led Frank to defeat and despair.

Elizabeth also saw in the reconstruction how her Mother, Diane came to the marriage from a poverty family filled with unresolved fears of not surviving. So when Frank lost his job the panic button was pushed in Diane. She resorted to blaming Frank which only crushed him the more. Elizabeth could understand for the first time how insecure her Mother was that caused her to be so punishing to Frank. A new appreciation and compassion grew within Elizabeth toward Frank and Diane. Elizabeth's hurt and anger shifted to feelings of sadness, compassion and forgiveness toward Frank. Elizabeth realized on a deep emotional level, since she was seeing all this acted out in flesh and blood before her very eyes and ears, how the horrors of the depression and the two family backgrounds allowed her parents to behave the way they did. They were doing the best they knew how under the circumstances. They too were trying to survive and feel good about themselves.

During the family reconstruction, Elizabeth was invited to step into the role of her alter ego as a child and confront her Mother in several scenes where Elizabeth was suffering conflict from trying to obey her and at the same time be independent. For the first time Elizabeth used her anger and frustration as a strength to confront Diane about her confusing double message. Diane backed off, realized what she was doing and gave a straight single message instead. The confronting led to good results. Simple as it was, Elizabeth experienced that she could get out of that bind. She could use her anger as strength and survive!

As we see this we can understand why Elizabeth was afraid of marriage on some unconscious level. She learned she had to make the significant others happy by pleasing while at the same time be independent. She also had learned not to trust men to provide for the family. This could only lead to no-win situations of great stress.

After the family reconstruction, when she experienced a way out of the bind, she felt safe in relating deeply. She would not need to repeat the old way. Her survival was not at stake if she did not please her new lover.

The power of the reconstruction enabled Elizabeth to transform the old dynamics into new ones that were now functional for her as an adult.

The power of a family reconstruction process resides in the fact that the process enables the Explorer to relive her childhood experience in a new way as if she were actually facing her real parents and family members. An altered state of consciousness is achieved when all the conditions are present as I referred to earlier.

However I have come to believe that there is even a more powerful dynamic at work. This process opens the door for the Explorer on the day itself or perhaps later on to accept ones parents as truly human. When this comes about within the Explorer, the Explorer gives a deep unconscious "yes" to his or her roots. In doing this, the Explorer becomes full. Being filled, the Explorer experiences new power, confidence and self esteem.

At least this is my experience. And I suspect this is why I enjoy doing family reconstruction more than sitting in an office talking to someone *about* their lives. Family reconstruction engages the person in the fullest sort of way psychologically.

Just as family reconstruction engages the full psychological system of an individual so does it engage the entire social-familial system of the individual, treating at least three generations. This is what one would expect from Virginia Satir. She really saw reality in its systemic whole. If time permitted I would love to write of how many ways Satir's approach differed from others because she was willing and able to deal with all the factors impinging on a person's life. I would like to create a new name for Virginia Satir's work. In the past it is referred to as "communication theory, or therapy, or model." I would call it an "eco-psychological approach to growth": "Eco," because it embraces all the factors surrounding the person, "Psychological," because it embraces all the internal factors within the person, and "approach to growth," because it is far wider and deeper than mere therapy. For example, I see family reconstruction more in the modality of spiritual growth than in the modality of therapy. Often my clients will want one-on-one therapy, but will not touch family reconstruction with a ten foot pole. To engage in the process of returning home again in a new way or completing the circle requires an inner strength which is a bit more than that required for individual therapy.

Virginia Satir's Process of Change

Laura S. Dodson

SUMMARY. This article describes Virginia Satir's theoretical base out of which grows the theory and practice of her process of change in psychotherapy. Her theory is set in a context of other psychotherapeutic theories and is described with case examples of application. Virginia's process of change is applied to individual, couple and family therapy particularly its application to cultural change is discussed.

I. INTRODUCTION

This article is intended to give the reader a clear picture of how Virginia Satir viewed the process of change in individuals, couples, families and larger systems. To give this picture, the reader will be aided by a brief understanding of her philosophy in a context of a broader context of other psychotherapeutic philosophies. These topics will be addressed briefly in the first part of this article.

The second part of the article will discuss what Virginia called, "The Ingredients of Change." This material is taken for the most part directly from audio and video tapes made of Virginia as she talked about the ingredients of change. In this part of the article the reader will gain a flavor of Virginia's warmth, related use of language, her deep acceptance of life as a process, and her respect for every person. Woven throughout the article, one will see the role of the therapist as teacher, careful listener, nurturer, and enabler to the change process; "leading the change process by following a half a

Laura S. Dodson, PhD, MSW, is Clinical Psychologist and a Jungian Analyst. She trained with Virginia Satir and co-worked with her over a period of 25 years. In May of 1988, 3 months before Virginia's death, she co-worked with Satir in the U.S.S.R.

step behind" (Satir, 1969). This section of the chapter will include practical application of Virginia's ideas through case examples.

In the last eight to ten years of Virginia's life, she became more and more aware of how her change model related to change on a world level. The last part of the article will relate her views of change to this broader perspective.

II. THEORY AND PHILOSOPHY UNDERGIRDING VIRGINIA'S PROCESS OF CHANGE

Anthropologists, historians, politicians, and psychologists have been intrigued with the process of change for generations. Though anthropologists like Victor Turner (1967) describe for us the elements of organic processes of change in tribes, change in more "highly" developed cultures has tended to be superimposed. A hierarchical model is most frequently employed. Virginia Satir's model of change is more akin to the anthropological descriptions of organic models of change, done however, in a more conscious way through her approach to psychotherapy and education (Banmen, 1987).

Psychotherapy in the West has developed as a science based on Newtonian physics emphasizing linear thinking and cause and effect. Western society has focused on division of thought and of professions. In this context, psychotherapy has developed as a part of the medical sciences. Linear thinking has been applied by the therapist as he/she looked for "the problem" and "the solution," the "illness" and the "cure."

Virginia's work is more related to the new paradigm of our time—the dynamic interrelationship of all things, life as a process, and the natural tendency of all things to move toward growth and wholeness. This way of thinking can be seen in the new physics and in quantum theory far more than in Freudian based psychotherapeutic thought.

Albert Einstein's quantum theory and other concepts in the new physics (Bohm, 1980) emphasize interrelationships and flow between all things. The ancient philosophies of Chinese medicine, Taoism and other eastern religions have for centuries seen things in wholes. Quantum theory has brought science toward a closer relationship with these ancient medical and religious perceptions and Virginia's work has brought psychotherapy in the same direction. Abraham Maslow, Sidney Jourard, Carl Rogers and Carl Jung are other early leaders in the holistic model of psychotherapy. Virginia Satir is the master of the simple, direct, practical and educational applications of holistic principles to human growth and development. Her work represents a break in traditional therapy. It relates more to eastern religious thinkers, new physics, and Jung than to traditional psychotherapy.

Virginia recognized that people *want* to grow and develop psychologically. The drive to grow and develop — Virginia saw this as *the* key drive above all the drives mentioned in Freud's drive theory. She believed that people have within them all they need to grow and develop. The task of the therapist is to assist them in awakening their *inner healer*, which is related to a Universal Wisdom. The medical model of psychotherapy views the patient as wounded and the therapist as healer. To Virginia, both the therapist and client are wounded healers. Life is a process of wounding, healing, and continual growth and change — a process in which we are all engaged. Though she was never a student of Jungian thought, Virginia's concepts of life as a process of growth and change will be recognized in Jung's individuation process. His work, too, reflects the dynamic relationship of all things and belief in the inner healer. Virginia saw growth and development of the individual intricately intertwined with that of his/her family of origin, ancestors and culture. The system of the individual's psyche took on meaning to her not only as seen in the context of ancestors and culture and the history of mankind but, as well, in the current context in which the person lived. Developmental stages were not unimportant to her but were only one "window" through which to see.

Though Virginia read Jung's ideas and other schools of thought, she never devoted herself to a study of others' ideas. She was interested in practical, every day education and application of truths that she discovered through life and work. She looked for simple words close to meaning to educate people about life and change. She saw psychotherapy as intertwined with education and firmly believed that education was a major ingredient in change, an essential ingredient to the development of a new consciousness.

Virginia Satir began her career in the helping profession in 1936 in Chicago, first as an educator and then as a clinical social worker. In her practical, common sense approach, her disagreement with psychotherapy of the day was simply based on the fact that she saw that too often "it didn't work."

She saw early on that schizophrenia did not operate in isolation. In 1942 she began treating the whole family of the schizophrenic. Virginia grounded her ideas in solid research in the late '50's and early '60's at the Mental Research Institute in Palo Alto, California where she worked with Don Jackson and Gregory Bateson. She aided Mike Murphy in his early development of Esalen Institute. Esalen represented to Virginia important efforts in the direction of innovations in psychotherapy in a growth model.

Foundation concepts behind Virginia's model for change were systems theory, life as a process, the inner healer in everyone and the need for education to aid change. As she began to formulate her ideas on the nature of the change process, Virginia designed educational models to help people through the process in growth enhancing ways.

As strongly as Virginia believed people have a basic drive to grow and change, she also believed that environments that enhance self esteem are essential to a healthy growth and change process. Growth enhancing environments can be described as providing respect for each individual, freedom for each individual to be aware of what they see, hear, feel, think and touch and to comment on all the data their senses give them. Virginia developed concepts and methods to teach therapists how to create a healthy environment to facilitate change. By 1967 she had developed a model for the change process and she continued to refine it throughout her life. She applied it to education, prevention, individual, couple, family therapy and world healing.

III. THE INGREDIENTS OF CHANGE

Change goes on all the time, most of the time unconsciously. For Virginia, the focus of therapy was conscious change.

Creating intentional conscious change is the essence of therapy. When people come for therapy they are asking for help to change. They may know the place where they want to go or they may not. The ingredients of change are identical whether we know where we are going or not. (Satir, 1972)

A. Stage I – STATUS QUO

The place where we are Virginia calls "status quo." It may be difficult, painful, even excruciating, but it is familiar and that gives a feeling of safety. We may want to change but we are scared.

When change is sought through therapy the motivation is usually from one of three things:

1. Someone wants us to change. They feel they cannot tolerate the way we are.
2. We see a vision of what is possible for us.
3. We are in so much pain that we feel change *must* happen.

These motivations are in conflict with the desire to keep the status quo. The familiar gives "survival comfort." Often it is the case that aspects of the status quo that are causing problems represent coping skills that were once useful. These coping skills helped the person or couple or family to manage what may have felt like life/death issues. They gave a sense of equilibrium or "survival comfort." People can only practice what they have learned. Their coping skills represent what was once their best effort to survive and what remains as coping mechanisms that operate out of consciousness and often with similar emotional intensity as in the initial painful situations. Until we become conscious of these coping skills, and how they operate, it is difficult to make change. Awareness of the "status quo" offer a baseline from which to make change.

Often there is so much fear in going beyond the status quo that we will "lie on a bed of nails or get beaten up . . . anything" (Satir, 1972). That is at least familiar. Going on to the unknown involves often enormous, intense fear, not unlike the initial fears we may have felt when the coping behavior was initially constellated.

Sometimes therapists try to deal with the fear by soothing their client. ("Everything will be okay.") Therapists sometimes make the error of trying to convince people they can continue in the present pain. That does no good. Another common error of the therapist is to try to reason with the person to get them to change.

("You got beaten up last night. I am sure you don't want that to happen again so you had better change something!") Such logical presentation of facts won't help either.

What does help is imaging the change desired. "The language of change is [a language of] pictures" (Satir, 1972). The unconscious does not respond to logical talk, image is its language. One needs an image to follow to help change occur. Usually before an image of a hoped for change can come, it is necessary for the client to feel safe enough to explore their fears and to have their fear heard. Often this exploration is in images as well. If the therapist focuses on the client's hope and fear, often we find that the person is afraid to even ask for what they want. "I can't get it even if I wanted it, so why hope?"

The therapist may ask, "Is there anything in you that disagrees with what you are saying about staying where you are?" "Do you have an image of that part of you? If it had a voice, what would it say?"

Once the fear and hope is acknowledged then the door is open for the therapist to move to the next step, still in the realm of imagery, not concrete ideas. The therapist can now ask, while extending themselves and their warmth and humanness to help make it safe to dream, "If you thought it would be safe to go after what you want, what would you *do*?" or

1. "If I visited you and the change that you want had happened, what would I see?"
2. "If you had a magic wand and could make one thing different in your life (in your family) what would you most want to make different? If that were different, how would that help you?"

Now the therapist needs to watch the body tension closely. "Reading" body reaction will help the therapist to know the depth of the fear. This awareness on the part of the therapist can aid the therapist in extending appropriate care and empathy to aid the clients in coping with fear. The therapist might then formulate, "A piece of you wants to change. We could join together to explore what could happen."

By such statements as these, the therapist aids in creating a nurturing, growth enhancing environment *in the therapy room*. This is a prerequisite to any change being able to occur. What the therapist says, *but even more* his/her attitudes and behaviors, sets this environment.

The therapist lends support to the side of the person that hopes and wants to make dreams come true. At the same time, paradoxically, he/she will lead by following a half step behind. The patient created the image for the hoped for change, taking the lead. The therapist believes that every person has within them all the wisdom they need to guide the change. He/she believes themselves to be trustworthy to take the journey all the way with the person to discover their inner wishes and truths and to walk through all the stages of change with them.

The therapist creates a nurturing environment, for we all need a tremendous amount of support to make conscious change. He/she gives room for the wish to be explored. The therapist operates on the premise that the client is doing the best they know how at that point in time, that they want something more and that they do not know how to make it happen.

In this manner, the therapist has suggested himself/herself as a partner in exploration. He or she has conveyed that there is no blame, that respect is there, and that there is room for the person to see, hear, feel, think and comment on his/her experience and be heard. These attitudes are demonstrated by the way the therapist is; not told to the client in lecture form rather shown by a way of being. Usually when this is done, people become more comfortable and the desire to change can grow.

The old adage is "discomfort makes people change." The therapist historically may not be so careful to make their patient comfortable. Comfort is not the same thing as accepting the status quo.

> All live beings are working toward a harmonious balance in themselves. It is only because of the "shoulds" and "oughts" that we put on ourselves that we stay in a bed of nails. I have never found anyone who stopped growth because they were comfortable. I have found people who get a little but then think they shouldn't ask for more. The belief that you only go ahead if you are anxious denies all the natural things about nurturing. (Satir, 1972)

"Shoulds" and "oughts" are, of course, a part of society's and parents' way of inculturating individuals. Virginia is concerned with the problem of self worth being based on behaving in ways that might have fit at one time, place, or situation and might not be useful at another. She is concerned with "shoulds" and "oughts" that have become a part of low self esteem and fear of taking risks. A quote from conversations with Virginia "I made up an old saying, 'To the degree we accept and value ourselves we can allow ourselves to grow and make the changes that fit with our growth'" (Satir, 1988).

Once the therapist has made a beginning partnership connection with the person, fear and hope have been explored, the person has allowed themselves to image change and they have experienced in the therapist and in themselves a growing attitude of respect and exploration rather than blame of self or other, more work can be done to aid the person in becoming more conscious of the nature of their status quo. We need to know where we are as a foundation to know where we are going. Usually the present is automatic and out of consciousness. To make explicit what is implied, or what is being lived out is an essential base for conscious change.

Some images Virginia used to clarify the status quo follow:

1. The therapist is aware that the status quo represents a sense of balance within a person and in their family system and environment. An image which the therapist might offer is a mobile in balance. This could be illustrated in a personal way by information the client has given about themselves and their family as their mobile in balance. There is balance even if the price is high. (Satir, 1972)
2. To illustrate in imagery the price of the balance Virginia sometimes spoke of a teeter-totter in which a heavy person is on one end and a light person on another. The heavy person sits close to the middle to make balance and doesn't get much of a ride. The skinny person must lean back. (Satir, 1969, 1988)
3. The client's position in status quo can be likened to feet being in concrete. They are standing up but they can't move. Such an image might evoke feelings of being trapped, stifled, frozen, or other feelings and descriptions from the client. (Satir, 1988)

The images Virginia used had a touch of humor and they conveyed no blame but rather a vivid description. They usually evoked a picture image in the client's mind and as well a body feeling. Each therapist can find their own style and own creative way to evoke images in the psyche that aid the client in learning, on a body and psyche level, and that teach in descriptive, non-blaming ways.

Once the language of imagery is catalyzed by the therapist, the client will begin to give their own images. These offer more precise pictures of their situation and can become an "incode" language between the therapist and client that carry far more meaning than any logical explanation of the situation could ever do.

B. Stage II – RESISTANCE

Stage II of the change process in therapy is characterized by resistance to change and further incorporation of the therapist. "In this stage the status quo is getting ready to re-shape" (Satir, 1988). Note Virginia's positive re-framing of resistance. Foreign elements (in addition to the therapist) are coming in – elements such as new information and the need for or yearn to change. The status quo equilibrium resists foreign elements; in the same way that the body in need of a transplant organ resists the transplant. The body needs the organ to live but the body tries to repel it. The wish to live is overcome by the unfamiliar. The "automatic" behavior and the "comfort" of the status quo has a survival sense about it. One may feel that change would be like death itself.

The individual psyche system has a life of its own and the family system has a life of its own. To continue its life in the same way, it must repel the foreign element. Repelling is the natural, even instinctual effort of the system to maintain its balance.

In therapy, this is called resistance. It doesn't negate hopes or wishes; it does not have to do with them. Virginia's approach to change can be contrasted to other forms of therapy that may mistake resistance as an unwillingness to change.

In Stage II, as clients resist, the therapist will likely be seen as a foreigner and at times he or she will receive anger and criticism from the clients. He or she may feel: "I am not good enough at my work"; "I'm not doing things right." An even more encompassing feelings can develop: "I am a bad person." (This is Virginia's "I don't count" position. See Barbara Jo Brothers' "Methods for Connectedness," this publication.) Or the therapist can feel: "The client (or family) is untreatable" ("they don't count" position).

If Stage II is to be successful the therapist must stand on his/her own feet with no personal investment as to the outcome of therapy, no need to gain esteem through feeling that they did good work, and with no need for reward. The therapist needs patience and vision and deep belief in people. The therapist moves to make contact with the part of the person that has hopes and vision and with their energy, however slight at this point, for change. At the same time, the therapist feels empathy and respect for the status quo and the fear involved in change.

An example of how these attitudes on the part of the therapist might be conveyed are:

1. Sometime we are caught between what we want and what we feel we ought. This can be illustrated with a client by having one person in a group pull on one of their arms and another person pull on the other arm (all three persons standing) so that the client experiences bodily the shoulds and oughts versus the wishes and wants pulling them apart. Immediately after this experience has "registered" in the person, revealed by his or her words and body, the therapist might ask what the experience was like. The therapist might generate a dialogue between the two aspects of the client to personify and objectify the pull. A third part, an ego observer "higher self" might be elicited for advice regarding the polar tension.

2. The therapist might say, "To even be here in therapy is an act of courage. You are afraid, you feel stuck but already you have one ingredient of change working for you: courage" (Satir, 1988). The therapist might go over (a) what went into the decision to come, (b) helping the client to re-image and own that they walked in on their own two feet and it is their desire to change, (c) their hope, however faint, and their courage that is shown — all this is an aid to help them claim their power. Realization of one's power can facilitate a move out of the status quo.

3. Another example of meeting resistance follows:

> Client: "I don't know why I ever thought *YOU* could help us." If the therapist hears the fear behind the statement he/she can respond, "You are afraid I won't be able to help you either. You fear that you *and* I will be defeated and you will feel lost and hopeless all the more." With such statements we have reached behind resistance to make contact. Usually once the feeling is recognized we can go on patiently, "following a half a step behind." (Satir, 1972)

To move through the fears that motivate resistance, we must make contact with the person we are working with so that we touch them on levels behind the resistance. To make contact we must meet the other person where they live, where their deepest feelings, hopes and fears are. They must know that we have been there with them without their having had to lose any self esteem to allow us to see. In fact, if full contact has been made, we have also met the "higher self" in the other. They know we have seen at least some of their potential as well. They feel *more* self esteem while at the same time they have allowed us to touch their woundedness (Satir, 1988).

C. Stage III – CHAOS

Stage III is characterized by chaos. While the Status Quo stage has predictability by rote or habit and there is a sense of control through the familiar, in Stage III there is no way to predict because everything is in the process of change. The old way of being is no longer comfortable and neither is there a new order. A crisis has been created by the therapy process itself.

Often a person might have entered therapy in a crisis or almost in a crisis. Their attempt is to maintain the status quo and to resist change. At the same time, periodically present is the drive that disrupts the status quo, opens the possibility for growth and change. Therapy moves toward and into the crisis. Most important in the crisis which is actually furthered by the therapy process itself is the relationship between the therapist and the client(s). The relationship is the container during the crisis.

Virginia saw crisis as an "opportunity for growth." A crisis can occur: inside the family system from events such as childbirth, aging, illness, and so forth; outside the system from events such as job loss, job change, economic depression, or war; and/or inside the *psyche* of an individual — urged by the depth of the psyche or the "higher self."

Crisis is not a problem which needs a solution nor an illness which needs a cure; it is a normal part of the process of life. Crisis is a *process* which, when recognized within a growth framework, can signal that support is needed to aid the person, couple, family, group to listen deeply to themselves. Such deep listening enables one to follow the process of change toward constructive outcomes, for images and pictures from the depth of the psyche are needed to guide the process.

To Virginia, crisis and the chaos that ensues is not a negative phenomenon but rather an important signal to tell us it is time to change; time to listen deeply inside ourselves for what the nature of the change is to be. However large or small the change, the crisis and chaos have the positive potential to wake us up to take another look at our lives within and without.

Crisis is an opportunity for opening to new possibilities and an opportunity for protecting the old way. If we protect against what is opened, we lose it. To be vulnerable is to be open. The job of the therapist is to create a safe place to be vulnerable.

In this vulnerability, the therapist directs the person toward their own inner truth. For example if someone proclaims to the therapist in the midst of the crisis, "I never want to see you again!" what the person needs is not a cathartic expression of feelings. The goal is not to discharge all the feelings, but rather, to discover the trigger that set off the feelings. To discover the trigger:

> I will often ask the person to simply breathe deeply and go inside after some deep breaths to see what feeling is there. Almost always I get, "I feel desperate, lonely, sad," or some such deep feeling that the person struggles with. This is the trigger that led to the explosion. Consciousness of the feeling that is behind the explosion gives the person a new awareness

. . . another foreign element that upsets the equilibrium the family had but also opens to new possibilities. (Satir, 1988)

Awareness doesn't all come at once. When enough has come that there is a break in the old status quo, the person can begin to play around with a new idea, a new experience. This freedom comes not from words but from experience and images.

The art in this stage is to keep a creative tension between resistances which are to be respected and at the same time explore openings which move toward new possibilities. Too often out of his/her own fear of change the therapist may err on the side of staying with the resistances. We can project that attitude and collude with the client's fear immobilizing both the client and therapist. Our awareness of our own fear, taking care of this problem within ourselves, and being conscious and empathic of the client's fear can give the therapist and the client the courage to walk into fear. This is core to how change occurs.

> In this time of chaos, I have a rule of thumb. No changes are to be made that cannot be executed in 10 seconds. In this stage the person moving toward change cannot rely on his/her judgment. This is not a centered stage. I give no validation to threats to separate or divorce, etc., as at the moment the chaos has not yet offered enough material for such decision. I regard such drastic decisions in this stage as statements of the self inside crying for what it hopes. (Satir, 1988)

The clients feel things are worse and often they are, at least on the level of symptom and disruption to status quo. What happened before that was problematic happens now in exaggerated ways. In stage I and stage II clients need to have explanation about how problems can be exaggerated for a time in a chaos period. This aids people in preparing for the chaos period.

In Stage III, the therapist models being fully present as the clients "run for cover." The therapist is totally present, giving in ways the people can feel safe and cared for. The main therapeutic intervention in stage III is the art of modeling by the therapist of walking with the client(s) into fear and simultaneously respecting the fear in supportive ways. The therapist remains centered in the #5 communication position — [Editor's Note: Congruent communication is the #5 communication response; see "Methods for Connecting" this issue] — gives, receives and checks out meaning, listens and makes room for everyone to be seen and heard. He/she is a "detective on the client(s) process" until they have gained awareness and have learned to explore their own processes. The therapist keeps a growth enhancing framework in the vessel of the therapy relationship, describing, not judging, the process. The model desired is a model for growth, not a model for blame.

An example of interaction in Stage III is:

> Husband: I am so angry at my wife, I feel like killing her.
>
> Therapist: You feel like killing your wife, tell me how.
>
> Husband: I'd like to choke her to death to stop her chatter.
>
> Therapist: Can you think of other ways?
>
> Husband: I'd like to smother her, stuff her mouth with rags.
>
> Therapist: It seems you are telling me you want to stop her chatter.
>
> Husband: Yes.
>
> Therapist: Oh, okay, maybe we can find some other ways to do that.
>
> Husband: Okay.
>
> (As the therapist begins to work toward that goal she addresses the wife.)
>
> Therapist to Wife: Do you know what he means?
>
> Wife: Well, I get angry and I scream at him a lot.
>
> Therapist: What do you get angry about?
>
> Wife: I talk to him and he doesn't answer. I just keep talking and still he doesn't respond so I keep saying, then screaming the same thing.
>
> Therapist: (Continuing to be a detective on the process in descriptive, non-blaming ways, assuming — *knowing* — that all behavior makes sense and searching for the sense) "Oh, can either of you remember a time when chatter happened and tell me what happened just before?" (Satir, 1988)

As the therapist continues to explore, she begins to see that just before the chatter the wife felt unappreciated, even expected not to be heard. The therapist may find that her behavior relates to past hurts, not only to husband. All the while this is going on, the husband is listening and gaining deeper understandings of what his wife feels. The wife may begin to learn to separate out her old hurts and present hurts. She may see new possibilities for asking to be heard. Husband may see that he had previously assigned his wife an intent in chattering which was to "drive me crazy" when really she had an entirely different set of feelings at the core of her motivation for "chatter." She feared she was not appreciated by him and she felt the pain of the present moment in which she felt unappreciated along with a long history of pain about not feeling appreciated.

Note that the therapist did not tell the man what to do. She/he didn't have to. He didn't want to kill his wife any more. He had new information about her and about himself. This broadened his array of choices. The incident, too, is taken out of a blame framework, feelings are honored, and it is put into a framework of new learnings, imploring meanings, and gaining new understandings.

Humor was an important ingredient in psychotherapy for Virginia, particularly in this stage. In regard to the couple in therapy described above, Virginia might herself role play for the wife. Her manner of doing this would convey to the clients a sense of being understood and accepted while at the same time, it would invite an observing ego in the clients, furthering their ability to image new possibilities of behavior.

An example of this follows:

> (Virginia is physically close to the husband, her face only about a foot away from his) "Listen dear, I have something to say that I want you to hear." (She waits for his eyes to meet hers and then, role playing the woman, says in a clear, direct way what she wants.) (Satir, 1988)

What emerged from this dialogue is the aspect of the wife which doesn't want to be heard because she fears exposure. Now hearing from a deeper level what goes on in the wife becomes possible.

It becomes evident at this stage that the *problem* is not the problem, but the ways of *coping* with the problem, which Virginia saw as the case in most situations. In this stage once again the therapist helps further the person's freedom to use all their senses and to comment on what they experience. This means asking as often as there is some nonverbal indication questions like "What are you feeling (thinking, seeing, hearing, etc.) right now?" "How do you feel about feeling (thinking, seeing, hearing, etc.) that?" The senses are the feedback system that help us to respond to the original problem. Such questions help the person have better access to their own internal feedback system that is their resource for problem solving. Undoubtedly they have been, historically, unheard or ignored in some way and have learned to ignore or pay insufficient attention to their senses, making the way of coping with the problem become the problem.

D. Stage IV – PRACTICE

By this time, good will has occurred between the therapist and family members, the individual in therapy or the group, as well as increased sense of good will toward one's self and between themselves. There is safety to practice new ways of being. Never mind if they are done "right." The idea is to experiment.

Our work in this stage is to take what is learned that is authentic about ourselves and our environment and bring this authenticity into awareness over and over again. It is very easy to forget something we have learned. We don't get good at tennis by thinking about it. We have to practice. It is the same with emotional changes.

In practice we will look clumsy and awkward. It is important to consider the ability to look that way as a badge of courage rather than something for which to judge ourselves negatively. Practice can take the form of reminding one's self through notes, diaries, pictures or notes on the mirror where they are seen often. It takes breathing deeply when we are anxious. It takes patience to continue to take ourselves back to our inner truth and remind ourselves of what we almost forgot in our anxiety and habit. Sometimes it requires living more slowly with more time to reflect for the practice period.

Family members, group members, and the therapist give loving support particularly in this stage to help people see in the moment what is happening, to change it and to note when they have behaved in changed ways. The therapist must be security for the person so they don't return to a survival stage out of fear.

The pain of Stage IV is a pain of recognition. There may be tears and pain but it leads to hope, versus the pain of Stage I. In Stage I the pain is one of blame of self and others and the situation. This pain leads only to closed doors.

IV. NEW STATUS QUO – NEW BALANCE

A new status quo is reached once we have practiced the new learnings. The new status quo contains our new or relearning of biological laws and learning one's own truth. This creates freedom of energy that has been bound and a releasing of creativity. Often when this occurs not only is one thinking clearer, but literal vision can be clearer. Energy level rises. The ability to make clear decisions increases. Harmony within the self and between self and other is increased. Often a connectedness to universal energy is felt — a sense of being "at one with" all of life.

This description of the ingredients of change is not intended to state that status quo is bad and change is good. There are, of course, times to maintain status quo and resist change. There are times when this itself *is* growth; times when sameness and predictability are needed to grow. The pivotal question is not change or status quo, it is the *state of being* behind what we do. Lethal to one's humanness is an internal or system status quo which is maintained out of fear and caution, forming an identity based on external rules of behavior and denial of one's communication with one's senses and inner truths. In this state psychic energy is blocked within the person. This contributes to blocked energy in all systems — couple, family and world.

On the other hand, status quo maintained to hold some aspects constant while others are integrated or created is indeed a part of the process of growth and change. We may be in a maintenance status quo form while we are making connections with the self or incorporating this information into our actions, decisions and connections with others. If we are really in connection with the self—freely using all our senses, and incorporating this information from self and senses into our actions, decisions, and connections with others—we are in a process of growth, even though we may be in a maintenance status quo form. The key to the growth process is freedom to have access to all of one's sensory feedback, to be conscious of this feedback, and to make choices for commitments that fit for the context rather than choices indicated by our conscious internal rules.

Summary of the Ingredients of Change

In metaphorical review, Stage I, the status quo stage, initially gives the feeling of our feet in concrete. The feeling is heavy but stable. At least we are not falling over. In Stage II the new element (be it therapist, new ideas, new images, new marriage, etc.) comes in, is resisted and—if the change process continues—the resistance gives way to Stage III, chaotic eruption to the old equilibrium. It is characterized by fear, extremes in behavior, crisis and new information. In Stage III, one foot is out of the concrete, the other set in it. We periodically fall over in the struggle and feel hopelessly caught. With courage, patience, and much support we break the other foot loose.

Stage IV is the practice stage. Both feet are more and more out of the concrete and we know we cannot return to the old yet there is instability in the new. The pain of this stage is more a pain of *birth* than the pain of Stage I which is the pain of closed doors in which one feels stagnant, numbed and dead. The two pains are to be greatly contrasted.

Stage V has the lightness one would feel to dance without concrete on their feet after dragging the heavy weight around for a long time. One's sense of well being and relationship to others and environment is enhanced. The old status quo identity has been to some degree based on automatic behaviors and identity has been more externally based. By Stage V there is a deeper trust in the self and identity is more within. To find truths and direction one consults more with the self.

Therapy is intentional change. Throughout the process of change

the therapist is steadfast, recognizes his/her common humanity —
that is that change is a process of life we are all in and that we all
fear. The therapist maintains his/her belief in the client having all
he/she needs to find their way and the therapist leads the process by
following a half step behind and by creating a growth enhancing
environment in the therapy process.

V. APPLICATION OF THE CHANGE PROCESS TO LIFE-LONG GROWTH

The stages of the change process repeat themselves throughout
life. Once we have gone through a process of status quo, introduction of a foreign element, chaos, practice and new status quo, the
cycle comes again. However, the cycle is progressive. To illustrate
this Virginia gives rough percentage figures to show movement
from immobilizing anxiety and fear to excitement and vitality.

The first time around there is 99% anxiety in the status quo and
1% comfort. In the new status quo there is 75% anxiety and
25% comfort. We are making the change but we are hesitant.
The past is still a pull. Though both feet are in the new there is
a question of how much we can depend on them staying there
in the new status quo.

The second time through the change process, there is less
chaotic feeling in the chaos and the practice and new status
quo brings 50% anxiety and 50% comfort. Up to this point, all
risk is fraught with anxiety and after this point there is at least
as much comfort or even anticipation as there is anxiety and
fear.

At the end of the third cycle there is 90% comfort and 10%
anxiety. Fear has been transformed into excitement and vitality. (Satir, 1988)

Then one's basis for life has been altered. Life becomes more and
more based on excitement and vitality instead of fear; creativity
rather than protection.

This cycle can go on throughout life. (See Chart I.) It is possible
to move on and on in cycles of change, living our lives and dying at

CHART 1

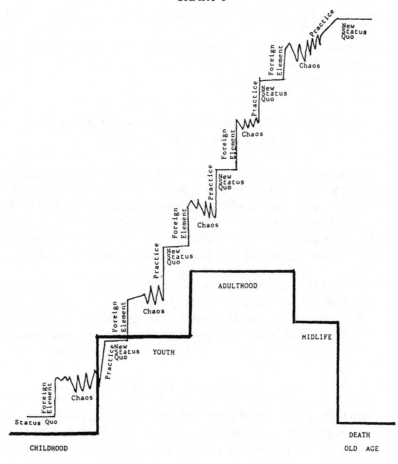

Linear Model of Life

Virginia's Model for Change as a Process Throughout Life
(Satir, 1988)

a peak of our creativity rather than dying our lives. In this state, we would find ourselves looking for another foreign element like one follows a wish or desire. We would find ourselves gaining in the freedom to take risk recognizing that we move to somewhere where we have never been. We would see that new place as fresh territory, providing new learnings. We would follow signals from our inner selves rather than living by rules to protect us from our fears. Chaos would no longer be chaos, but would be part of the energy of life and experienced as peak experiences, as Abraham Maslow put it.

This growth model for life and change is contrasted with the more classic model of life that we have been taught, a linear model. This model is indicated by the thick line on Chart I. Basically it is that childhood, youth, adulthood, old age are the stages of life. We wait for the next stage with caution and fear. While in one stage we cautiously make preparation for the next one the focus of our life, making it difficult to experience the present moment. Such an approach avoids and contains our fear. Human beings are capable of shifting to a model for change at any age.

VI. CHANGE IN INDIVIDUALS RELATED TO WORLD PEACE

Virginia saw psychotherapy as facilitating intentional change. She saw that the process she described in therapy was also a process of life itself within individuals, in couples, families, groups, and cultures. She had the belief that more and more people were moving away from linear models and into growth models. She had the hope, that enough people making the change would change world consciousness. The following are quotes from fall of 1987 and spring of 1988 from Virginia:

> There is a new energy and new forms in motion (in our world) I am a representative of that. I do not want to die with the world thinking that what I did was unique to me. I have tried in many countries to assist people in becoming more human by being deeper in touch with themselves and becoming conduits for connecting and giving and receiving (and by living in a growth model). If enough human beings move into a growth

model for change we would move into a new (planetary) consciousness that has never been present in our world before. Instead of a linear model of life that pigeon-holes us into youth, adult, middle age and old age, or pigeon-holes us by our label of work or our collection of material things or what color we are or where we live, people would become each wonderful manifestations of life. They would not be boxed by Mrs., Dr., Mr. or Ms., young or old. The soul within would find a voice for its growth and its unique expression.

If nations met nations with this attitude, meeting with fear and protection would not be the focus but rather we would have the ability to use all our senses to take in what is and comment where we choose.

When I speak of peace within, peace between and peace among, I am not thinking about how Jordon and Israel can get along but I am thinking about how I can be with you and you with me.

I have a passion about me since I was five years old. That passion is "people can evolve." If we don't live what we are talking about we become liars.

Your presence on this planet (at this time) is essential to creating change. Your consciousness is needed.

VII. THE LEGACY

Virginia lived to see and describe her process of change and the role of the therapist in the process. She applied her process of change to clients, families and groups and to all human beings. She saw it as a normal process of life. Often she was a teacher and therapist for therapists. She assisted them in becoming more human and tending to their own growth process — living what they taught.

In the last 10 years of her life and particularly the last four she applied her process of change to world peace. Among my last conversations with her (in the U.S.S.R. in May of 1988) her mind was intensely at work on looking at the evolution of consciousness in our world. The intent of world leaders like Mussolini, Hitler and Lenin, and many before them was to create a better world for all people. Despite their intent, to a large extent, the opposite occurred. After she researched history more, Virginia planned to write more about these observations. She believed even the best intentions would not create a better world. A new consciousness is required.

In her lectures in the U.S.S.R. Virginia spoke of the new consciousness containing a freedom for women from their confined roles world over. She spoke of the needed freedom of individuals to travel and live wherever they chose. In each lecture she pointed to evolution of consciousness on the most personal level and created an atmosphere for people to meet as people in the room.

As Virginia was on her death bed it was my task to organize in her absence the program she had planned to do entitled "What Heals the Family Heals the World." Rianne Eisler became the keynote speaker for the event telling us about the absence of the feminine in consciousness which she had researched historically. Rianne sees this as a major factor in change on a world level.

Virginia was a representative of new energy. Had she lived on, I believe she would have championed the simple language and practical, everyday ways to teach the new consciousness necessary for world change. Her genius was in bringing such essential awarenesses to the general public in words close to meaning that touched every one where they lived.

I believe that the cutting edge of psychotherapy, be it individuals, couples, families or groups, is to take what we have learned about the change process and apply it to raising consciousness within all cultures, all age groups, all socio-economic groups. The changes on earth that are now occurring can, through such application, be made from a dramatically different consciousness than that of our forefathers. The new energy of which Virginia spoke can be catalyzed beyond therapy. Virginia's principles can be taught, lived and modeled to transform human consciousness. The result will be prevention, not only in families, but in whole societies — prevention on a cultural scale. In a word, world peace.

REFERENCES

Banmen, J., Gerber, J., Gomori, M. (1987). "The Virginia Satir growth model." A study guide on becoming more fully human. (Available from John Banman, 11213 Canyon Crescent, North Delta, B.C., V4E 2R6).

Bohm, D. (1980). *Wholeness and the implicate order*. London: Routledge and Kegan Paul.

Satir, V. (1969, May). *Process of family therapy*. Speaker. Fort Logan Mental Health Center. Denver, Colorado.

Satir, V. (1972). *The change process*. [videotape] Kansas City, Missouri: Golden Triad Films, Inc. (Available from Ray Price, 3422 Coleman Rd., Kansas City, MO 64111).

Satir, V. (1987, Fall). Lecture. [cassette tape] Vista Hermosa, Quernavaca, Mexico. (Available from Morris Gordon, 6509 Waterway Drive, Falls Church, VA 22044-1328).

Satir, V. (1988, Spring). *The change process*. [videotape] Gabriel Island, Canada. (Available from Nancy MacDonald, 17918 23rd Lane, N.E., Seattle, WA 98115).

Turner, V. (1967). *The forest of symbols, aspects of Ndembu ritual*. New York: Cornell University.

Peoplemaking:
Self Esteem or Shame?

Maxine West

SUMMARY. Virginia Satir recognized self esteem as the culmination of identity development within a nurturing and validating environment. The proposition of this author is that the shame-based identity, on the opposite end of a continuum from self esteem, is the culmination of identity development within an invalidating and contemptuous environment. The perspective presented here is generic and comprehensive, using the established work of Satir on self esteem and more recent work by other published authors on the subject of shame. The development of the shame-based identity as well as the dynamics of the shame-based family system will be presented and explored.

Virginia Satir, in her work on self esteem, has written, "feelings of worth can only flourish in an atmosphere where individual differences are appreciated, mistakes are tolerated, communication is open, and rules are flexible — the kind of atmosphere that is found in a nurturing family" (Satir, 1972, p. 26). She says, " I feel that if I lived in such a family [a nurturing one], I would feel like a person in my own right — noticed, valued, loved . . . " (Satir, 1972, p. 13). She describes a most complicated process, the development of an identity based on self-esteem, with a simple notion — that self esteem thrives in a nurturing environment. In other words, we will know and believe that we are lovable, if, and only if, we were nurtured and loved by our parents. Elaboration on the meaning of

Maxine West has been in private practice for ten years. Her work on Shame-based Family Systems is in press (Minneapolis: Comp Care).

Correspondence concerning this article should be addressed to Maxine West, MA, Clifton Oak Therapy Center, 337CH Oak Grove, Minneapolis, MN 55403.

"a nurturing family" could be, and of course has been the subject of many pages, books, and journal articles. Satir writes and talks about what some of this "nurturing" entails. In order for children to have a high sense of esteem, parents need to provide validation of their child's growing abilities and accomplishments. They must validate their child's sexuality and right to care and respect. They must validate their individuality. According to Satir, individuals who have received adequate love and validation will be people who know that they are lovable, know how to take care of themselves physically and emotionally, are comfortable with intimacy, and are able to get along well in society. In short, these individuals will possess self esteem. The task of analyzing the etiology of self esteem is enormously complex. The various dynamic processes and forces that operate throughout the development of the individual to contribute to esteem, are complicated, intricately interrelated, and sensitive to timing. Yet, Satir's simple explanation that the development of feelings of worth requires a nurturing environment renders the complex task of understanding self esteem in human and readily understood terms.

I first wrote about what I called the shame-based identity and the family system that helped to create it, in 1982. I consider the development of this type of identity to be the result of dynamic forces that are similarly complex to the forces that result in esteem. However, I see the shame-based identity as being on the opposite end of a continuum from an identity based on self-esteem, as shame thrives in an environment that is diametrically opposed to the environment that nurtures self-esteem. In other words, we will believe and know that we are unlovable, if and only if, we have been treated with shame and disgust by our parents. I think that it is important to distinguish two distinct forms of shame. First, shame is a basic human emotion that we are equipped to feel at birth, and which is a normal part of the human experience. The shame-based identity, however, is something that we are not born with and that is not common to all humans, but is the result of years of identity formation in which the shame affect has played a central role.

Silvan Tomkins' (1987) pioneering work on affects is extremely thorough in its explication of the first kind of shame. Tomkins sees shame as one of nine innate biological affects, the others being interest-excitement, enjoyment-joy, surprise-startle, distress-anguish, anger-rage, fear-terror, hunger and dissmell. Like the other affects, shame is a biological response to one's environment, involving physiological change. Tomkins postulates that arteriolar dilation, which accounts for "getting red in the face" when shameful, and hormonal changes, which may account for the "shut-down" that people report, are intrinsic to the affect of shame. He proposes that neurohumoral vasodilators which are triggered quickly produce "cognitive shock" and thought confusion almost instantly, while the lingering of the hormonal changes creates a lengthy "shut down" or break in the experiencing of the self, despite all efforts on the part of the individual experiencing shame to reconnect with the self (Nathanson, 1987).

I believe that Tomkins' (1987) biological approach to understanding the affective and behavioral experience of shame offers important validation for the humanness of the shame experience. From this perspective, we can understand that it would be as impossible to control one's experience of shame and blushing under certain circumstances as it would be to control one's experience of hunger under certain circumstances. We can examine shame as a natural and useful part of being human, rather than as a pathological psychological defect. Tomkins' work sheds light on shame as an important mechanism in the learning process of children. Shame can be viewed as one of the ways that the values and mores of a culture are instilled in the individuals of that culture — that members of a society achieve socialization and learn to fit in appropriately with groups of others. Individuals who seem incapable of this affect stand out in their selfish, rebellious and "shameless" behavior. Shame occurs in the context of interaction with others, especially important others. The affect of shame is experienced when the person we interact with "mirrors" back to us disgust, contempt, displeasure, hate or disrespect. The more important the other person is to us, the more we are at risk for shame. Keeping in mind the powerful motivating force of being liked and being loved for all humans and especially for children, the power of the shame affect is understood more fully. The shame experience has been variously described as feeling unlikable, unlovable, rejected, abandoned, unacceptable, and disgusting. The experience is a potently negative one and leads to learning to avoid experiences that may evoke the shame affect, accounting for its socializing potential. If the child is acting in unacceptable ways or is breaking societal norms or mores, disgust may be the appropriate parental response, helping the child to disengage from that behavior. For example, if a child is hitting his infant sibling, the appropriate parental response to this unacceptable behavior is horror, which will evoke shame in the child, and is a necessary learning experience for the child. Given that we have the innate biological capability for the shame affect, and given that we are social creatures who interact with others, we are constantly at risk for experiencing shame. In this form, the shame affect is a simple response to the kind of social interaction we are having. If we are behaving unacceptably and are treated with distaste by another human being, we can feel shame, and it is appropriate and in line with the reality of the social interaction.

However, we are at risk for shame whether or not we are behaving unacceptably, because the shame affect is evoked by the response of the significant other, not by the behavior itself. So, as an example, if a woman is raped, shame is an appropriate affect, for indeed, rape is disrespectful and humiliating treatment by one human being to another. However, the rape was not evoked by any unacceptable behavior on the part of the woman. Similarly, if a child showing their drawing to their family is teased and belittled, the child is apt to appropriately feel shame. However, the family's humiliating treatment was not triggered by any unacceptable behavior on the part of the child. Hence, vulnerable children are dependent upon the ability of their significant others to appropriately and accurately mirror their behavior back to them, which accounts for their vulnerability to developing a shame-based identity in the absence of a nurturing parenting environment.

This second form that shame may take involves the entire identity and is a somewhat more complicated response to one's environment than the shame affect. The shame-based identity, as I have called it, indicates lack of self-esteem, inability to feel loveable, and inability to believe that one is worthwhile. An individual in this state is not necessarily responding to the quality of their interactions or treatment by others any longer, as the shame has become independent of outside "mirroring." The shame-based individual can experience shame even in the face of positive and accepting interactions. Critical to the development of a shame-based identity is the quality of the relationship between children and their worlds. The shame-based identity is the result, I believe, of our parent figures mirroring back to us that we are inadequate, disgusting, unlovable, dirty, bad or defective. The mirroring process is the same process that Satir writes about when she describes the validation and nurturing that result in self-esteem, except that parents who nurture self-esteem mirror mostly respect, approval, and caring rather than shame and disgust. Incidents that induce shame are part of the childhood of everyone. These isolated and necessary events of shame are not sufficient to induce an identity based on shame. Typically, if there are but isolated experiences of shame, then there are also more consistent experiences of love and respect. However, if the relationships of the child are ones that provide consistent disrespect, the affect of shame that is induced by these kinds of interactions becomes central to the identity that is developing in this young person. Once the child's experience of self has been sufficiently influenced by the shame affect over the duration of years, the child comes to believe that the reality is that they *are* unworthy, defective, unlovable, and untouchable. The child absorbs the "mirroring" and the shame affect as if it is an accurate reflection of who they are. They begin to develop a cognitive reality that reflects what their affective reality has been. Examples of cognitive formulations that follow the shame affect are; "I never do anything right," "No one could possibly like me," "I am stupid," "I am too quiet," "I am too loud," "I make everyone angry," " I am bad," "I am too fat," "I am too thin," and "I cause everyone trouble and am not worth it." This list could go on to include many more statements that are negating and indicative of self-hate. While some of what the child was told overtly is absorbed as part of the cognitive content of the child's beliefs about themselves, I believe an equally important portion of the negative belief system is based on the affective response that is evoked in the child by the quality of their interactive experiences.

Once the identity has been founded upon the cognitive and affective base of shame, it is not readily changed. An individual's reality within the early developmental environment forms the basis of their core feelings and beliefs about themselves. Since the shame condition is extremely painful, the shame is not readily brought out into the light to be examined or shared with another person. Shame-based individuals believe that they are truly defective and it is too shameful and embarrassing to admit that one has this kind of defectiveness. The shame, therefore, prompts the hiding of the shame through isolation, withdrawal, and shying away from intimacy and care. These protective maneuvers aid the shame-based person to keep the shame intact. Potentially corrective experiences, experiences where the person is valued and accepted, are eliminated due to the protective stance of keeping the defective self from further exposure. Intimacy requires self exposure and sharing of feelings and needs. The shame-based individual believes that "who they are" and especially their own needs and feelings are "wrong," "bad" and "not worthy" of anyone attending to. When it is remembered that this individual as a child was consistently shamed for who they were and how they were feeling and for what they were needing, it is easy to see that the shame-based adult is going to fear that they will again be shamed by these new others, for who they are and for what they feel and for what they need. This is an agonizing position to be in. The shame-based individual is still craving and wanting to be loved and is hoping that they will be able to be accepted and to accept self. However there is a hopelessness and a trap for the shame-based person. They have the concrete "truth" of the early life that is "fact" for them, that their being is unacceptable and unlovable. The attempts to correct have all failed. There is no way for them to make up for their "primal" unlovableness.

When two shame-based individuals come together and begin to form the foundation of a new family system, their shame identities have a profound impact on their relationship styles and abilities and on their parenting styles and abilities. In their relationship to each other, both individuals desperately want the other to be able to love them and want to receive the validation that they missed as children. However, both individuals are saddled with the firm self-perception that they are in fact unlovable and unworthy. The shame identity, as was earlier stated, is protected and denied by strong defenses, so the shame remains a secret. Though hidden, it exerts a powerful effect on the quality of interactions between the couple. The prime defense protecting the shame from exposure is avoidance of shame-inducing experiences, so these two individuals develop a set of unspoken rules about what is to be allowed. Needs and feelings are powerful areas that lend threat to shame-based individuals. Consequently, they fear their own needs and feelings as proof of their unlovableness and badness and fear the other's needs and feelings as proof of their inadequacy as a partner. A shame-based individual has long since learned that if their loved one is in emotional pain or is in need of something that it is only because they were not attending to their partner correctly. Their loved one's needs or feelings are proof that they are not "good enough," they are inadequate to love the other "right," triggering the experience of shame. When one is defending against this kind of shame, one sets up patterns and rules to disallow needs and feelings. Intimacy is injured and both individuals fail to receive or give to their partner. The relationship is experienced again as another confirmation of their individual failure. The original bargain was that they would validate and love the other, in a sense make up for their partner's lack of being loved as a child. However, this bargain fails, because of the secret of each partner's shame, the denial of that shame, and the rules and patterns that are set up to protect the individuals from shame exposure.

When these two adults fail in their couple relationship, they do so with shame and with rage, which are intimately connected. Rage is one of the reactions to the shame affect that acts as a barrier or wall to keep others away, and in so doing, to protect oneself from further exposure. Out of the rage often comes physical and emotional violence or the "silent treatment" or at the very least intense blaming of self and other. All of these behaviors are humiliating and disrespectful, inducing shame in oneself and in the other. Confirmation of the well known affect is experienced when the pattern from the family of origin is repeated. The atmosphere in the shame-based environment is tense and a sense of failure is felt by both members of the couple. It is not a satisfying or nurturing environment. Both people are needy and feeling more hopeless about deserving love. They feel failed both in their families of origin and now in the new relationship. Communication is fragmented, angry, and defensive.

At about this time when both have given up on the hope of being valued and loved, the first child is often born. This child is coming into a family where the two adult parents are feeling discouraged, have a shame-based identity, and have sets of rules and behavior patterns that are aimed at protecting themselves from having their hidden shame exposed. The child is entering a family system that is shame-based. The dynamics and the interactive patterns that are established have been established directly in relation to the shame. This child is at risk for shame, simply because it comes equipped with needs and feelings, the very equipment needed to expose shame. Satir identified the need for parents to validate their child. The child's sense of esteem is dependent upon the parents' ability to communicate an understanding and acceptance of the child's feelings, needs, accomplishments, abilities, and sexuality. It is an impossibility that these two shame-based individuals are going to be able to give the child these "supplies" since these are the very things that they have identified as shameful in themselves. As parents, their child's needs and feelings are likely to be received as an attack by the child on the parents' competence. The parent is likely to react to the child out of that shame, by shaming and attacking the child. For example, if the child is scared and comes to the parent and the parent tries to "fix" the child, but the child remains afraid, then the child may be told that they are a cry baby, and that the parent will give the child something to really cry about if they don't stop the crying. This reaction by the parent comes out of the shame-based belief that if the child loves the parent then the child will be comforted by the parent's efforts. If the child cries, then the parent is a failure. The fact that the child is fearful at all can be perceived by the parents as proof of how the parents have failed, as they tell themselves that if they were good parents and attend to their child properly, their child would never be afraid. These kind of distorted and unrealistic beliefs are rampant within the shame-based system. The child growing up in this system inherits these kinds of impossible beliefs, cognitions that arise out of the shame-base, and cognitions that in powerful ways perpetuate the shame. For the child, who is developing a sense of who they are, these interactions and beliefs induce consistent experiences of shame. They experience shame when they are feeling sad, hurt, angry, afraid, and perhaps when they are feeling joy. They can experience shame about their accomplishments if the parent ignores them or belittles them because the accomplishment is not perfect, usually meaning that it is the accomplishment of a child and not of an adult. Mistakes are not learning experiences in a shame-based family, but are a source of shame. The belief is that you should be perfect, and that mistakes expose. Mistakes leave you at risk for blame in this family system. The result of these kinds of interactions is to leave the child in consistent ways, experiencing the shame of themselves. The need for nurturing, valuing, and acceptance is not fulfilled. The need to be loved is unmet, but very alive and powerful. This child grows up with that same shame-based identity and the same kinds of defenses and shame-based beliefs that the parents grew up with. The cycle is set in motion to pass to the next generation.

Shame as an affect is a part of the experience of all human beings. It is an affect that results when a human being treats or interacts with another in ways that are humiliating, disrespectful, belittling, contemptuous, abusive, invasive or rejecting. The more important the person is to us, the more likely the shame response. While painful, the affect dissipates. The shame-based identity, on the other hand, while related to the shame affect, is not a part of all of our experience, and is immeasurably more pervasive and destructive. The same unit of humiliating social interaction that induces the shame affect, when repeated over and over again in a fairly constant way with a child, produces the shame-based identity. The shame-based identity is founded upon shaming treatment by one's parents over the course of years, while one's sense of identity is forming. It would be correct for the shame-based person to conclude both that the shame is an incorrect perception of themselves, and that the shame is an absolutely accurate reflection of the kinds of experiences that they had throughout the important years of development. Developing awareness about the roots of their shame constitutes the beginning of a way out of the shame for the shame-based person. It offers a way to understand the strongly felt shame within the core of their identity as an accurate reaction to the environment that they grew up in, but not an accurate reflection of who they are. This understanding lends a way to loosen the destructive grip of shame, allowing healing to occur in its place.

For an individual with a shame-based identity to achieve this freedom from shame requires an enormous battle on the person's part and is a formidable undertaking. The very core self believes in and has had confirmation of their unworthiness and defectiveness. The person must wage battle against their own sense of truth. I believe that professional help is almost always essential for waging this battle effectively. Shame-based individuals, when children, learn to see themselves through the eyes of their parents and important others in their world, like all children. The shame-based parents are individuals whose own shame-base distorts their vision, so that what they see in their children is not a true vision of the child, but a picture of their own distorted worth or shame. Their vision is clouded, distorted, fragmented, and their children grow up with this inaccurate reflection of themselves carried as truth. The adult must find another who has accurate vision to begin to see themselves through the clear reflection of this more accurately "sighted" person, the professional helper.

Virginia Satir inspired my work on the shame-based identity, because she recognized the powerful influence of a child's reality within the early developmental environment on identity formation. While she wrote about the development of self-esteem, it was but a short leap to carry her understanding of developmental dynamics to apply to the development of the shame-based identity. Though Satir does not directly talk about a shame-based identity, her work on the importance of parental validation certainly suggests examination of the result of lack of parental validation. She describes parents with the clarity of vision needed to reflect a child's reality back to them accurately and appropriately which validates them and builds self-esteem. My work examines the results of inaccurate parental vision, a view that is clouded by shame, which leads to invalidation of that child, and to the building of their shame-based identity. Although the enormity of the shame-based dynamic can feel overwhelming, my clinical and personal experience have shown me that healing and a building of esteem is entirely possible for those individuals who can patiently commit themselves to the process of uncovering the roots of their shame.

REFERENCES

Nathanson, D. L. (1987). A timetable for shame. In D. L. Nathanson (Ed.), *The many faces of shame* (pp. 1-63). New York: Guilford.

Satir, V. (1972). *Peoplemaking*. Palo Alto, CA: Science and Behavior Books.

Tomkins, S. S. (1987). Shame. In D. L. Nathanson (Ed.), *The many faces of shame* (pp. 133-161). New York: Guilford.

West, M. (1982). *The shame based personality: A look at the process of identity formation and development*. Unpublished manuscript. (U.S. Copyright obtained 6/13/86).

Experiential Learning:
Reflections on Virginia Satir
and Eugene Gendlin

Bala Jaison

SUMMARY. The following article is about three things: my impressions of Virginia Satir's work, my personal experience of her, and the profound connection between the work of Virginia Satir and Dr. Eugene T. Gendlin's Focusing work.

My attraction to both of these great teachers is not surprising. They both share a type of wisdom which in metaphysics is often described as "intelligence lovingly applied."

In this article I hope to convey what I see as an organic and compatible overlap between Satir and Gendlin which will hopefully be useful to the readers of this publication.

I chose to write this paper on Virginia Satir, because her work and being have been a model and inspiration to me both personally and professionally — and — while I am learning a great deal, at this point in time, from non-experiential approaches to family therapy, for the purpose of writing a paper, I feel most familiar and closely aligned with her work. It also interfaces remarkably well with the

---

Bala Jaison, PhD, is a counselor and psychotherapist in private practice. She is also a scholar in the field of metaphysics, especially as it relates to transpersonal psychology. She is the Director of Focusing for Creative Living in Toronto, and the Educational Consultant to the Focusing Institute in Chicago. She has authored a number of articles on the creative applications of Focusing and has had several articles published in the Journal of Esoteric Psychology on the applications of Focusing in transpersonal psychology and metaphysics. She is currently involved in an intensive clinical extern program sponsored by the Family Research and Clinical Project of the Children's Aid Society of York Region, Ontario, Canada.

Bala Jaison can be reached at Focusing for Creative Living, 282 Erskine Ave, Toronto, Ontario, M4P 1Z4.

Focusing work of Eugene T. Gendlin, Ph. D. with which I am also familiar and closely aligned. I find the overlap and inter-connectedness between the work of these two teachers intriguing and very relevant to the field of family therapy (I will elaborate further, later in this paper).

I was first introduced to Virginia Satir's work in the early 70's and subsequently met her four times during the 70's. Each time was in the context of large group work ranging from 20-500 people. In each meeting I was awed by her perception, humor, and ability to captivate and magnetically hold the attention of an entire audience from beginning to end—she was absolutely compelling and charismatic. She had a way of including every single person in the audience no matter how large the group, and an uncanny ability to make each person feel that she was talking directly to them.

I remember being struck by some of her maneuvers, like tying people up with ropes to demonstrate how we get bound and wound up in our personal scenarios, or sculpting a family in various postures. She used stools and chairs or boxes to put children at the same height as the adults, placing them eyeball to eyeball in order to communicate with more equality. These methods have now become legendary. At the time I thought they were ingenious—they were!

My personal experience with her was this: I had been introduced to her at each of the first three workshops I'd attended. We met again for the last time in Scotland in the late 70's. It had been at least four years since the previous meeting. She was wandering around the speakers platform as some 500 people began filing in, in dribs and drabs, to the huge theatre—in-the-round.

Our eyes met. She walked directly over to me, took both of my hands into both of hers and greeted me like a long lost friend: "How are you my dear, and how is your work going?" I was stunned and certain that she had me confused with someone else. I felt very embarrassed and for a moment, didn't know who to be, myself or who I projected she thought I was! Seeing the look of total bewilderment on my face, she immediately referred to something we'd discussed in our last encounter. I was astonished. It seemed impossible that she could remember me. I felt so validated and truly valued in that moment, that all I wanted to do was cry and cry and cry. Instead, I further confused the issue by averting her eyes and pretending that I didn't feel what I felt. She was so brilliant at dealing with other people's non-clarity and confusion. I can't remember what exactly happened in the rest of that encounter, but I had the very good fortune of being able to process the experience with her later that day. Again, I felt touched to the core by the intensity and caring with which she listened and reflected my feelings of discomfort. I learned more about good therapy in that encounter than I had from hundreds of pages of reading.

Her work and being were influenced by a number of factors, common of course, to all human beings: family of origin, personal relationships, life experience, etc. I suspect however, that there were two particular factors that contributed to who and how she was, both personally and professionally.

The first had to do with her height. According to an article by Richard Simon in the *Family Therapy Networker*, (1989, p. 37-38) she was both a sickly and awkward child, having reached her adult height of nearly 6' by the time she reached puberty. I believe she may have experienced herself as different, odd, and always an outsider. Consequently, she was deeply sensitized and drawn to others who felt the same sense of oddness and separateness. Her empathy in this regard, always drew her to the underdogs and outcasts of society, e.g., schizophrenics, unwed mothers, the institutionalized, etc. Her strong sense of compassion and understanding of people's foibles and peculiarities is evident in her films, books, and especially in live demonstrations. This type of empathy is never for show — it can't be put on — and thus it added to her realness.

The second factor was her personal philosophy which she brought to everybody. I believe this was the cause for some of the rifts between her and her colleagues. She was a deeply spiritual woman and therefore concerned with such things as self-realization, centeredness, inner alignment and attunement to her deepest Self.

This inner attitude translated into intense interest in people and in educating them toward their own inner process, self-esteem, and self-worth. This was carried out by constant positive feed-back, reflecting the good (or goodness) in people and validating them and their deeds, wherever possible.

She therefore spoke in terms that were much more spiritual than clinical (to the consternation of many of her peers). In Richard Simon's 1985 article in the journal "Common Boundary" she says about her work:

> When I am completely harmonious with myself, it is like one light reaching out to another. At the outset, it is not a question of "I will help you." It is simply a question of life reaching out to life. All life talks to life when it is in a harmonious state. If my ego is involved or if I need them to get well, then it is a different story. This is one of the secrets of what I do, if there is a secret. (Simon, 1989, p. 39)

This is not therapy talk, it is pure metaphysics, although she did not use that term (to my knowledge.) She did however express her interest in evolving consciousness, both individual and planetary, and made mention in her workshops of "the Path," a spiritual term for each person's dharma or way. It would stand to reason that her work, her interactions with people, and her way of life would reflect her personal philosophy.

To my knowledge Satir never mentioned Eugene Gendlin. Certainly, though their teaching styles and form of presentation differ, they share an attitude of deep respect for people and life. (It may be of interest to note that both were influenced by the work of Carl Rogers.)

Focusing is based on the idea that each of us has a place inside that knows something, in the sense of rightness (like fresh air) or inner wisdom. This knowing place when contacted, is experienced in a bodily felt way and is different from, and often in contrast to, what is intellectually or analytically perceived.

A distinction should be made here between the Focusing *process* and the Focusing *attitude*, for they are different though intertwined. As a process Focusing has specific steps. It involves paying attention inside to something:

- not yet clear
- but distinctly bodily felt
- connected to something in one's life
- which produces steps of change when stayed with in a gentle, friendly, non-judgmental way

The above is unique to Gendlin.

The Focusing attitude is a way of being with both self and others characterized by: gentleness, acceptance, non-judgement, non-criticism and respectfulness. It is a way that allows and permits whatever is there (inside) to speak freely and openly in an environment of safety.

The *attitude* is common to both Gendlin and Satir, and is also found in many current growth oriented philosophies.

Focusing, especially as it integrates into psychotherapy, makes every attempt to connect people with this inner knowing or core place. It does this by:

- Acknowledging whatever emerges (feelings, thoughts, images, words) in a most respectful and non-critical way.
- Listening in a way that is empathic, reflective and supportive of bringing the client closer (experientially) to his or her own process and intrinsic sense of subjective truth.

   (Gendlin takes the Rogerian reflective listening and builds upon it into what he calls "experiential response" which not only reflects what has been said, but points to the underlying "felt-meaning" of what has often been left unsaid.)

- Attitude: There is way of being with people that both Gendlin and Satir share. In the simplest terms it might be called genuine lovingness. In more complex terms it might be called genuine understanding. It is also called innate wisdom and cannot be taught, only learned by the direct experience of living.

The following is a 12 point list of what I consider the major characteristics contributing to Satir's uniqueness and style. I have pointed out the places where I see a particularly strong connection with Focusing.

1. ACKNOWLEDGEMENT: No matter how far-fetched or outlandish a person's ideas or feelings were, she acknowledged their point of view, letting them know they had been *heard*. (*This type of acknowledgement is intrinsic to Focusing.*) The result was that people felt included by her instead of left out — particularly useful in family therapy.

2. FEELINGS: All feelings counted. They may have been misplaced or misdirected, but if they existed, she emphasized owning them and making space for them to be there. "Making a space" for

feelings and attitudes, no matter how negative or awful, is identical to Gendlin's "focusing attitude."

3. PRESENTNESS: She was always in the present moment with people, what Ram Dass referred to as the "here and now" (way back in the 60's) and she asked for that same presentness from her clients. This is well demonstrated in a session described in *Satir Step by Step*.

In the session the husband and wife are very stuck in their lack of communication with each other. After much going back and forth, and bringing in Satir's famous element of touching, the husband finally admits that the experience of being in physical contact with his wife (under Satir's direction) feels "warm and fuzzy." When Satir asks the wife how it was for her, she begins to go into past history, thereby invalidating the here and now experience. Satir responds by saying: "I want you to look at me now, and I want you to listen very carefully. There's a bit of history. . . . and I have a hunch that you often times don't see what's right in front of your nose. . . . you almost did it right now . . . tell me what you feel . . . right now. . . . " The wife admits that right now it feels warm to her too. This is such a clear description of how she differentiates between what was and what is.

4. COMMUNICATION: Heightened communication, messages both verbal and non-verbal, and clear "I messages" were a hallmark of Satir's work. In her book *Peoplemaking* she devotes chapter after chapter to exercises that will help people communicate more effectively.

5. TEACHING and INSTRUCTING: While some therapists at times share insights and points of view, she was really a teacher, not just when actually teaching, but in the context of a therapy session. She actually was a teacher and principal before becoming a social worker and I suspect that teaching was a natural modus operandi for her—she did it constantly.

6. RESPONSIBILITY and OWNING: She frequently used the words "my sense of it" always owning her feelings, then checking with the clients to see if that was right for them. This is very different from interpretation or implication that the therapist must be right or infallible. She in fact stressed that something inside them already knew the way and she followed their lead. (This is also part of the Focusing philosophy.)

7. TOUCHING: There is not much new to add here since her physical contact with people is legendary, and often 'touching' (!) as in the film *Of Rocks and Flowers* where she has the children touch her face, which she does to them as well, and which they in turn do with their step mother. I feel that the whole issue of physical contact during the therapy hour involves a subjective and personal choice, relevant and appropriate to ones personal style, and the type of therapy being employed.

In the Focusing work we rarely, if ever, touch people while they are in process, yet frequently make physical contact e.g., a hand squeeze or hug afterwards.

Satir's commanding physical stature, plus her warm earthy quality, made her touching people seem as natural as breathing.

8. STRAIGHT FORWARDNESS AND DIRECT COMMUNICATION: Her questions to the family during a therapy session were direct and straight forward and she tried to get people to respond back in the same manner, emphasizing and drawing out not only what they thought, but what they felt and how they acted.

9. CONGRUENCY: This again is like Focusing, i.e., what a person says needs to match body language and inner attitude. In all of her books, there is strong emphasis on what the listener is left with when he or she experiences incongruency from the speaker. This is one of the main thrusts of her teaching, and also "in sync with" Gendlin's philosophy.

10. CREATING INTENTIONAL AND CONSCIOUS CHANGE: Satir was a master at helping people to choose change. She never undermined the often experienced feelings of fear and resistance around the "felt sense" (a Focusing term) of change. Rather, she validated those scared and uncomfortable places, and then gently and lovingly stayed with people through the often arduous process of transformation. In this respect she offered herself as a guide, mentor, and support system for those about to cross over the threshold into new states of awareness and consciousness.

11. REFRAMING AND POSITIVES: Virginia Satir is known for her ability to find the positive and growth steps in almost any situation. She was highly skilled at reframing situations so that everyone came out looking like a winner, e.g., making a dominating father into a very concerned parent. She always separated a per-

son's behavior from their being, thereby validating their intentions and goodwill.

12. LOVINGNESS: Her empathy, her compassion, and genuine caring for humanity is quoted over and over again by both her peers and friends. She truly believed that the world could be transformed through love: both self love and shared love, and seemed to live her life out of an attitude of loving service. Gendlin holds the same view and it is ever present in all of his work. Thus, the "Focusing attitude" (mentioned earlier) is the foundation upon which the rest of his philosophy is built.

I would like to end here with a story that I don't believe you will find anywhere else in print.

This takes place in Northern Scotland in an Educational "New Age" community called Findhorn. Satir was there for a number of days teaching about awareness in many different forms and guises, but the following unplanned teaching was the best. She stood up in front of the whole assembly (some 500 people) and said something like:

"I know all of us here are intensely interested in consciousness and human development. It is for this reason that I would like to talk about toilet paper! . . . specifically the toilet paper in the Ladies Room in the main lobby . . . I don't know much about how it is in the Men's Room . . . but . . . I have noticed for three days now that the roll on which the paper hangs is finished, and there are several more rolls stacked up on the floor, but no one in this *very caring, conscious, co-operative community*, can seem to find the time or energy to put a fresh roll of toilet paper on the roller!" We exploded with laughter and squeamish embarrassment; not one of us had failed to notice this and not one of us had done a thing about it . . . let the next one do it! "So, I'm wondering," she continued, "who exactly you think is going to do this? God? The Angels? The Magic Maid? Who?" The speech went on and on and became increasingly funny and serious at the same time. It was a profound spiritual teaching.

This event made a huge impact on my understanding of taking responsibility, and not dumping my share of work on others. I have since taken the time to put fresh toilet paper on rollers all over the world!

In closing, it seems that Gendlin, who works primarily with individuals, has taken the skills of listening, combined with his astounding ability to bring people to the most profound levels of their own depths, and not only turned them into a fine art, but has made a large part of his work immanently teachable (specifically taught in the six-steps of Focusing).

Satir takes what Gendlin so brilliantly teaches and models it, naturally and organically by her very presence — and, she not only does it with individuals, but with couples and families as well.

I feel that the integration of Gendlin's work with Satir's could be extremely valuable in the practice of family therapy.

REFERENCES

Gendlin, E.T. (1981). *Focusing*. New York: Bantam Books.

Rogers, C. (1961). *On becoming a person*. Boston: Houghton Mifflin Co.

Rogers, C. (1951). *Client centered therapy*. Boston: Houghton Mifflin Co.

Satir, V. & Baldwin, M. (1983). *Satir step by step*. Palo Alto, Ca.: Science and Behavior Books.

Satir, V. (1972). *Peoplemaking*. Palo Alto, CA: Science and Behavior Books.

Satir, V. (1972). *Conjoint family therapy*. Palo Alto, CA: Science and Behavior Books.

Satir, V. (1983). *Of rocks & flowers* [Video tape]. Kansas City: Golden Triad films.

Simon, R. (1989, January/February). Reaching out to life. *The Family Therapy Networker*. p. 37-43.

Satir's Formula
for Therapeutic Endurance:
The Wonderful Human Being Myth

Michael D. Spiegler

SUMMARY. Of the many factors that accounted for Virginia Satir's ability to create change in intransigent couples and families, the *sine qua non* may have been her therapeutic endurance (ability to "hang in there" with tough clients). Satir's formula for therapeutic endurance was her constant belief in the intrinsic worth of each individual — the wonderful human being myth — and its corollary that all people are capable of changing.

Many ingredients went into making Virginia Satir the outstanding therapist she was. One was her cogent conceptualizations of human nature and family dynamics (Satir, 1972, 1976, 1983; Satir & Baldwin, 1983; Satir, Stachowiak, & Taschman, 1975). Another was her personal qualities as a therapist (and human being). She possessed keen observational skills, an ability to clearly pick out the forest from the trees (even in the densest and most tangled jungles of interpersonal relationships), and empathic understanding. These qualities have been given special note in the numerous tributes to Satir since her death in 1988 (e.g., Andreas, 1989; Corrales, 1989; Simon, 1989).

Among the myriad therapeutic principles and techniques Satir used and taught to others, I believe that one factor is the *sine qua*

Michael D. Spiegler, PhD, is affiliated with the Department of Psychology, Providence College.

The author would like to thank Margaret Ann Waller, MSW, for her helpful suggestions on this paper. Reprints may be obtained from the author at the Department of Psychology, Providence College, Providence, RI 02918.

165

non of her brilliant success as a therapist. It is Satir's ability to "stay with" the most difficult cases, the seemingly intransigent couples or families. Clearly, the quality/skill, which I call *therapeutic endurance*, is not unique to Satir; it can be observed in many dedicated psychotherapists.

Therapeutic endurance is an essential quality/skill that needs to be emphasized in training therapists of all persuasions, but effective strategies for teaching therapeutic endurance have yet to be developed. The practical significance of therapeutic endurance to successful therapy — indeed to keeping "difficult" clients in therapy — is stressed, and its ethical ramifications are emphasized. Such information alone, however, is often insufficient to engender therapeutic endurance. It does not tell the beginning therapist *how* to "hang in there." To assume that it would is analogous to applying will-power to a tempting situation and is likely to be as ineffective as admonitions to "use your will-power" and "try a little impulse-control." The key to teaching therapeutic endurance may be to provide a simple formula that a therapist can easily follow in the midst of the frustrations arising from patients who try the therapist's patience.

Satir's simple formula for maintaining therapeutic endurance was her belief that *every person is a wonderful human being*, that each individual has intrinsic worth. The corollary of this fundamental proposition is Satir's conviction that all people have the ability to change their behaviors.

I can recall my initial reactions the first time I heard Satir say, "Everyone is a wonderful human being." The assertion ran counter to my knowing people who are clearly not wonderful, or at least whose *behaviors* seem to be the antithesis of "wonderfulness." Furthermore, the statement that "all people are wonderful" appeared naive in making an artificial distinction between people and their behaviors. Thus, it was tempting to conclude that what may have been Satir's fundamental axiom is both inaccurate and romantically-naive (Daniels, 1988; Liebert & Spiegler, 1990, Chapter 17). It was easy to dismiss the axiom, thinking that it was unnecessary ornamentation for an already attractive package of Satir's otherwise practical procedures for creating change in couples and families. But after observing Satir at work with families, the centrality of her axiom became clear.

Satir's consummate therapeutic endurance was based on her fundamental belief that all humans are wonderful and capable of changing their behaviors. The ultimate "truth" of Satir's belief is irrelevant. Satir's proposition is a myth, but like many personal and cultural myths, it serves to motivate and guide our actions (e.g., Bagarozzi & Anderson, 1989; Campbell, 1988; Watzlawick, 1984). The wonderful human being myth allowed Satir to not only "hang in there" but to continue to function at her highest level of therapeutic skill at all times.

REFERENCES

Andreas, S. (1989). The true genius of Virginia Satir. *The Family Therapy Networker, 13*, 50-54, 56.

Bagarozzi, D. A., & Anderson, S. A. (1989). *Personal, marital, and family myths: Theoretical foundations and clinical strategies*. New York: Norton.

Campbell, J. A. (1988). *The power of myth*. New York: Doubleday.

Corrales, R. G. (1989). Drawing out the best. *The Family Therapy Networker, 13*, 44-49.

Daniels, M. (1988). The myth of self-actualization. *Journal of Humanistic Psychology, 28*, 7-38.

Liebert, R. M., & Spiegler, M. D. (1990). *Personality: Strategies and issues*. (6th ed.) Pacific Grove, CA: Brooks/Cole.

Satir, V. M. (1972). *Peoplemaking*. Palo Alto, CA: Science and Behavior Books.

Satir, V. M. (1976). *Making contact*. Millbrae, CA: Celestial Arts.

Satir, V. M. (1983). *Conjoint family therapy* (3rd ed.). Palo Alto, CA: Science and Behavior Books.

Satir, V. M., & Baldwin, M. (1983). *Satir step by step: A guide to creating change in families*. Palo Alto, CA: Science and Behavior Books.

Satir, V. M., Stachowiak, J., & Taschman, H. A. (1975). *Helping families to change*. New York: J. Aronson.

Simon, R. (1989). Reaching out to life. *The Family Therapy Networker, 13*, 36-43.

Watzlawick, P. (1984). Self-fulfilling prophecies. In P. Watzlawick (Ed.), *The invented reality: How do we know what we believe we know? Contributions to constructivism*. New York: Norton.

An Essay of Virginia Satir

Birgitte Winkel

SUMMARY. A description of how Virginia Satir's theories of family structure and self worth influenced the work of a Danish social worker in her work with families in pain and in her teaching.

Virginia Satir came into my life at the right time in Copenhagen in 1969. After having learnt the ideas of Virginia Satir: that "Communication is the method and the goal of family therapy," I could not just continue in my traditional role as a social worker. Together with my husband Leo Andersen, a psychologist, we established a "Center of Therapeutic Communication." Here we worked as family therapists and gave many courses to social workers, psychologists, doctors, pedagogues and other professions who were working with problem families. I am thankful to Virginia Satir. She gave me the courage and background to work independently from the social security system, because I felt that we had more freedom to change traditional ways of treating problem families not being a part of the system ourselves.

The most difficult thing was *not* to focus at the I.P. and looking more at the family homeostasis than the concrete problems presented by the family. Her ideas of seeing the family as a sculpture is pure genius. Our tradition in teaching was "talking about" or explaining the theories in words. Often with the result that the students get bored and unengaged. By using her methods of movement in the group, showing and experiencing the pattern of a family sys-

---

Birgitte Winkel, Danish social worker, family therapist and body therapist, is in private practice in Copenhagen. She is also teaching staff groups in managing and open communication. She is a co-author with Leo Andersen of: "Familieterapi—hvorfor, hvordan?" *Gyldendal* 1985, and is author of: "Arbejdsglaede—personaleudvikling" (Joy of working—staff development), *Gyldendal* 1989.

169

tem, this gave another insight and understanding of how to change roles and rules in the family.

Virginia Satir taught us in very simple, clear and practical ways the ground rules of communication. Her use of humour and common sense made her easy to follow and very convincing due to her enormous practical experiences working with families in pain. Virginia Satir taught us: the therapist is herself a model of clear communication, and to join a course in family therapy after the model of Virginia Satir means that the participants are personally involved and responsible for their communication.

Working with the families using the model of Virginia Satir meant for me a new way of seeing my own contribution to the family in trouble. Now I saw myself as a change agent using the resources of the family, and it was the family itself who delivered the material that was worked with. Instead of the traditional patronizing attitude therapists and social workers tend to practice I liked the open forum Virginia Satir created where she put equal importance to every member of the family whether it was a child of three years or the dignified father. The therapist herself is a catalyst giving equal space for every member joining the session. She has given a precious gift to the therapists by teaching us how to give value to every member of the family, and how to support the family in taking responsibility for their own lives, instead of being "treated" by the professional helpers.

In all the teaching and treating families of all economic and social levels, Virginia Satir taught me that the crucial factor in what happens both *inside* people and *between* people is the picture of individual worth that each person carriers around with him — she called it "his pot." "Integrity, honesty, responsibility, compassion, love — all flow easily from the person whose pot is high. He feels that he matters, he has faith in his own competence. He is able to ask others for help, but he believes he can make his own decisions and is his own best resource. He accepts all of himself as human" (Satir, 1972, pg. 22). For me as a human being and as a therapist this knowledge is a base from which I can use my own intuition and creativity. I see it as my main task in my personal work and in my work with other people to learn and to teach how to get the feeling of worth. Satir taught me: start with yourself and others will gain. Satir also made this important statement:

I am convinced that there are no genes to carry the feeling of worth. It is *learned*. And the family is where it is learned. You learned to feel high pot or low pot in the family your parents created. And your children are learning it in your family right now. (Satir, 1972, pg. 24)
This is the essence of all that Virginia Satir wrote and talked about.

As a consequence of this philosophy it did not surprise me to read her last book "Meditations" (1985). It is written in quite another style than her former books. Here she pays attention to the physical body, to the breathing, sensing the body, the nature and the universe. In little simple poems she talks to another level of our conscious being. She helps us to relax and to become open to the ever-present life-force. She shows us her positive view of life, and she gives of her rich and generous being.

I wonder whether this gifted and unusual woman had a feeling that her days were counted?
She finishes her little book with the following:

As I leave you now, I leave you with tears — tears of joy that I've had this time with you. I see on the horizon more love, more relevance, more real cooperation, and I thank you for having joined me in this way. Now, when you are ready, say goodbye to what we've had and hello to what can happen.

Farewell. (1985, pg. 73)

I am thankful to all she gave me: A fuller and more conscious daily life with my own five children, with my husband who is also my colleague, with my parents, sister and brother. And she showed me a meaningful direction in my professional career as a family therapist and as a change agent in staff groups.

REFERENCES

Banmen, J. & Gerber, J. (Eds.). (1985) *Virginia Satir's meditations and inspirations*. Berkeley, CA: Celestial Art.
Satir, V. (1972). *Peoplemaking*. Palo Alto, CA: Science and Behavior Books.

Healing Virginia

Barbara Jo Brothers

Virginia was actively engaged in *living* almost to the very moment of her dying. As partial testimony to that essential life-oriented attitude so characteristic of her, I share this account: my part in working with Jean Houston on healing Virginia.

I am motivated to add my account of this particular sequence because I think Virginia's dying was consistent with her living and her teaching; she believed in the power in choice. Her initial active engagement toward her own healing was so reflective of the essence of that great being we knew as Virginia Satir. Virginia was aware that there are cases of people whose cancer has gone into remission and vanished. She had more faith in possibility than do many of us—maybe most of us. Ever looking at the positive possibilities, Virginia, I am sure, might have thought that if even *one* such person had existed, there was no reason why she could not be the second one. She had, after all, her own theories about the emotional factors in the etiology of cancer (Brothers, 1987, 1988). There are people alive today with whom Virginia had served as therapist; their cancers have not killed them yet. Jean's mission, in working with Virginia during her last weeks, was healing/wholing; by no means was it simply an effort to "bring comfort to the dying."

Jean had enormous respect for Virginia. They did not know each other well; their paths had crossed at various meetings. They had worked together on at least one committee. Virginia had told me of one occasion where she had entered a room during a lecture Jean was delivering; Jean had stopped mid-lecture to acknowledge Virginia's entrance. But none of the path-crossings contained any occasions in which they got to *know* each other well. Charged with helping Virginia turn around her own immune system to activate her own healing processes, Jean wanted me to help her think of

173

images that would speak to Virginia. At that point, Jean was in telephone contact with Virginia twice daily, leading her in healing meditation. Images tailored specifically to Virginia would be quite valuable.

Jean Houston had called me when she learned of Virginia's illness.

"I know how much you love her — I just couldn't have that information without being sure you knew about it too."

The next day, not quite out of shock, but at least able to put two thoughts together, I had called Jean back.

"Is there *any*thing I can do?"

There was. I could provide those Virginia-specific images.

We would not tell Virginia of my participation as ghost-writer. We wanted to avoid any possible risk of diluting the power of the potential healing. Of course, I would have liked for her to have known and I would have liked *not* to be a part of deceiving her in any way; however, I wanted much *more* for her to become one of that small number who survive malignancy. It would be difficult enough. Few there are who can believe such healing is possible.

We had both grown up in the country. I simply took those rural images that I had heard Virginia use and put them with Virginia's own concepts, lightly coating them with some of the thoughts I had heard from Jean — the ones which had seemed to me to run parallel with Virginia's anyway. Jean had eagerly called me back after using the first script, requesting more — Virginia had responded deeply and with enthusiasm. It is no real wonder, I said. They are her own words wearing slightly different dresses.

The words I gave Jean for Virginia:

This is not your cancer. It is your mother's. She did not know how to let go of it but you do. She did not know she had another *choice*. You can make that other choice.

The other choice is to be *open*. To let Love *flow* through. Let your *system* open, *really* open, to whatever love is there in the moment, in all the moments, the full richness of the moments . . .

Fire the guards. You needed them when you were a little girl; you don't need them now. You have grown too big to need those kind of guards now. You are safe now. You have made whole systems like new. Now you can *allow yourself to take the next steps.* Let the rest of yourself evolve.

Like light on the cornfields — like the breezes rustling through the husks — the wind blowing the chafe away —

My [Jean's] voice is bearing the Wholing/Loving/Living/Healing Life from the ages. Let my [her] voice shine through all your *cells* — Let that Life sweep away the *wild, uncontrolled growth* . . . Receive your next 30 years here on this planet. You are not finished yet. Let the *reconstruction* of your deepest innermost parts take place. Something in you is trying to *grow*. Let the cells that don't need to be there get out of the way, let them be plowed under so they can come back the kind of growth that is *congruent* with who you really are.

Let the matter that is in those cancer cells be transformed into the blaze of loving *energy* that can sweep you into your new form.

You need the courage to open that deepest door.

*   *   *

Love is struggling for a deeper fuller birth, stuck in your cells. *Spirit* is trying to be born of flesh —

Let the trust open those last heavy doors. Let the warmth that is born in *real connecting* melt the membranes so the protein and minerals in all those cancer cells may be released back into the fertile grounding of your lovely body. You need the light and the heat of the energy held in those cells.

Let the warmth of the Spirit that moves across the waiting earth touch the very deepest parts of you — Let the Breath of Life blow away the shadows. Release the fear and be as a little child again, receiving . . . receiving . . .

Your *wholeness* has packed together into the cancer cells. Like a *seed* waiting for Spring's warm, moist light. Let the Light pour deep into you like the morning sun on a freshly plowed field.

Loving, living Life wants the growth. Join hands with . . . join hands with the spirit of Christos and Sophia and love the growth in you into its right form. Cherish the rampant spirit in those wild, uncontrolled cells and *consciously* grow that love. Attend to your insides so the form can make the shift. Attend and listen carefully: you are safe now, you are deeply loved, you are being re-woven.

Allow the reconstruction of all your lovely *parts*. Allow the opening, allow the connecting. Give every new little cell the guidance it needs to find its right place in your body.

Lovingly attend every little part of you so that it might find the role toward growth.

The Spirit is pouring through my [Jean's] voice now, the Holy Spirit flowing, making new, washing clean, purifying, making whole—The Holy Spirit of all growth, of all of creation, of the oceans and the Heavens comes through me [Jean] now—The Love that passeth all understanding—no need to understand; just open and receive.

You've not been afraid to *take risks in your own behalf*. Take the risk of feeling the full range of your rage about what put you in this spot—feel the full range of your feelings.

*   *   *

Why did Virginia respond to these images—her own recycled back to her from me, one of her fondest followers? Because she believed in the power in the possibility of *choice*. Because she understood *systems* and the vast differences between open ones and closed ones. Because she understood the importance of living *now* rather than thinking, "I'll be happy when . . . " this or that happens. Because she knew that bad choices for growth come out of bad early childhood experiences.

Virginia was caught by the very wonder of Life itself—a *cell* was a miracle. *Reconstruction* was what she was about, *congruence* was the method.

> I am fascinated with cells. I know we have still not yet probed the depths of all the cells . . . There is only one time in any living being that two cells unite. Only once. When the egg and sperm come together, that is the beginning of what is going to happen. Every cell thereafter comes out with two parts. It comes out with a total picture of the whole being and with its specialized part. If we look at that in terms of human beings, when the egg and sperm come together, we come out. We

don't come out half; we come out as a whole being . . . It only happens once they come together.

I have never seen a live cell under a microscope; I have seen pictures of it. One day I want to look at a live cell — I don't know how, but I will. I know that it is very, very tiny, perhaps so tiny that we would have to amplify it many times to see it. In that tiny, tiny thing — let's think of it the size of the head of a pin and I think that is a thousand times too much — in that cell is everything that is going to be your teeth, your breathing, etc. The two cells united are going to be your hair color. My god, think about it! In that teeny thing! You can put millions of them in your hand. Now, can you think of anything more mysterious and magic than in that teeny, tiny thing is everything you are today? Brilliant! I don't know whoever made this up!

. . . Hanging on for many people is survival, but it is actually death, premature death — because I fill myself up with all this stuff that is no longer useful. When cells can not allow themselves to die, there is no room for anything else. The biological parallel has a psychological face. It has a universal and a spiritual face because this is all the same. We have just changed the names. (Satir, 1987 tape 7)

Thus I laced her own words and concepts, that the robust seeds of her own genius might lift her back to physical wholeness. Or so I would have had it go; Virginia believed in the possibility and knew the power in her own work. Instead, she made her choice for the sooner date with Eternity.

And if the song sung her to sleep instead, at least the lyrics were shadows and shimmers of her own sweet song, sung back to her.

In Passing

In passing may the last thought in my mind
Be nothing shallow and yet not too deep
But something such as happy children find
In dreams that bring a smile into their sleep.

(Robert Lee Brothers, 1976, p. 65)

REFERENCES

Brothers, B.J. (1987). "Independence" *avoids* intimacy: avoidance of intimacy
    kills. *VOICES: the Art and Science of Psychotherapy, 23*(1), 10-23.
Brothers, B. J. (1988). The self-contained patient is the cancer patient. *The Psy-
    chotherapy Patient. 4*(3-4), 227-241.
Brothers, R.L.(1976). In passing. *The Lyric, 56*(3), 65.
Satir, V. (Speaker). (1987). Avanta Process Community VII, Module I. (cassette
    recording #7). Crested Butte, Colo: Blue Moon Cassettes.

The Dying Process
of a Conscious Woman —
Virginia Satir

Laura S. Dodson

SUMMARY. This article relates the author's experience with Virginia Satir in the last eight days of her life. The detail of incidents and interactions is most revealing of Virginia's ability to deal with such a poignant time in her own life in an open, focused manner and in a process like she taught others. There is a strong spiritual and human quality that the reader will find deeply moving.

Virginia said she wanted "the world to see my death as a success." At first I hardly knew what she meant. With time the meaning of these words is fuller. I feel she taught me how to die, and that she wanted to pass her learnings about this, too, on to others, just as she passed her other learnings about life to the world. It is too rare in our culture that one is invited intimately into another's dying process. Her life *and* death have had deep, transforming meaning. Each person who shared her dying process, in an intimate way, has their own story of her. This is the one I experienced.

In May of 1988 when she was working in the USSR Virginia had more energy than anyone in our crew of six. Virginia remained fully focused on the work in each of the four cities where we lectured and did workshops, while the rest of us took more time to rest. She spoke and worked with families with great clarity and the people seemed to hear her message deeply. She made further steps to

Laura S. Dodson, PhD, MSW, is Clinical Psychologist and a Jungian Analyst. She trained and co-worked with Virginia Satir over a period of 25 years. In May of 1988, 3 1/2 months before Virginia's death, she co-worked with Satir in the U.S.S.R.

relate what she knew so well in family healing to world healing. It was well received. Often, she seemed more inspired to do and say her message in a simple, clear, direct way than I had ever heard her in the 25 years I had known her.

She had no idea of her illness. Only two days before we left did she have a single pain. This was in the pancreatic area and a massage eased the pain. We assumed she had some of the parasites I suspected I had. On return when she learned it was confirmed I had parasites, she, too got some Flagil, and for a time continued to assume her increased pain was related to parasites.

In her usual style, Virginia was home only two days before she was off to work again, this time to lead the annual Avanta Conference (an organization that she founded and led, composed of people who do her work over the world). As she honored the older members, she announced here that she intended to live to be 102!

A week later, after doing a short TV program in Denver in route, she returned to Crested Butte for her summer training program that she had been conducting for eight years. It was there that her skin began to turn yellow with jaundice, she became very weak, and was taken to the hospital at Grand Junction, Colorado. She learned that she had a blockage in the pancreas and a cancerous tumor was suspected. She decided to return to her home in Palo Alto and go to the Stanford Medical Center.

I met her in Denver at the airport where she had changed planes. She sat exhausted in a wheelchair that had been rolled to the gate. We had planned to meet in the Red Carpet Lounge, but she paged me to come to the gate instead. "I could have never gotten there. Laura, this is the greatest challenge of my life. I don't want to *lose my life!*" She bent over in pain after the energy it took for her emphatic statement and mumbled, "And I wonder when I have such pain, why am I fighting for my life?" I had the strong feeling that she would die. After a few minutes I asked, "What would you like from me?" Her response was, "Come when it is right." We both knew that meant we would each listen deeply and when the psyche gave the word to me or to her, we would know, and I would come.

During the next seven weeks, I worked on the program she had planned to do in August, and was going to call "What Heals the Family, Heals the World." When it was obvious Virginia could not be keynote speaker, I called kindred spirits who might be keynote speaker. Those calls signaled some of the people who needed to hear of Virginia's illness. I reached Stan Grof, Bernie Seigel, Mary Catherine Bateson, Gerry Jampolsky, and Jean Houston. None could come to lecture but all telephoned Virginia with loving messages most important to her. Jean Houston did not know Virginia well, but it seemed clear to me that she should call Virginia also. "Are you sure, Laura?" "Yes, I am sure. You helped Margaret Mead when she was diagnosed with the same illness and Virginia needs you." Jean called and Virginia asked her to call daily. She did. Virginia felt calm and enriched after these conversations.

It was Rianne Eisler who responded to our need for a keynote speaker, and how appropriate. During our time in the USSR, Virginia and I had been looking through history at the many examples of leaders who had hoped to create "better" governments, but whose attempts ended in as painful a situation as had been present before. We had tried to put a historical-psychological perspective on this painful reality. We spoke in the USSR of the need for greater consciousness and incorporation of the emerging feminine consciousness as keys to world healing. Rianne, in her book *The Chalice and the Blade*, had historically documented the lost feminine. What a fine link to have her accept coming in Virginia's place.

Another speaker was Craig Barnes who was an editor of *Breakthrough* when it was being written jointly with persons from the two countries and published in English and Russian. He shared human stories of the process of the developing connection with Soviet and U.S. colleagues as they struggled to tell the truth in this book. M'Lou Burnett who had coordinated and shared our trip to the USSR came; she and I led the experiential part of the workshop.

Despite her illness, Virginia was actively interested in the development of this workshop. It was important to her. She kept having people call during the workshop until she reached me to see how it went. She was delighted and said, "Remember, little seeds like this grow." Her voice grew weaker. She told, over the phone, her dismay that she could not now even care for her smallest physical needs.

At Stanford, Virginia had been told that the cancer had spread to her liver as well, and that she could have radiation. This would

possibly give her six months to live, while without it she would
have two to three months. She chose not to have the radiation. She
decided to work with natural healing methods, such as cleansing
diets, natural vitamins, and minerals.

During those weeks, she struggled with what she needed to learn
from her illness, with her wish to write, and the probable inability
of her body to allow that, and with her other many losses.

In late August, I awoke one morning with a poem to Virginia. It
contrasted this time in her life with the time when she was five years
old and almost died with an erupted appendix. Her Christian Scien-
tist parents were reluctant to take her to a doctor but in the last
moment her father grabbed her from her mother's arms and took
her. This wound and this fight — for life — refined the richness and
depth of the healing ability that would be her life's work. As in the
finest historical traditions of healing, it made her a "wounded-
healer." Now, she comes to death's door again. This time the task
is surrender . . . not fight. This task is equally significant in her
journey . . . again a wound that brings powerful transformation has
come into her life.

I struggled for several days about whether to share this intense
dream-like message with Virginia. When she was fighting for her
life, how could I be so presumptuous? When I felt I must call her,
quite unexpectedly she was awake and alone, and wanted to receive
my call. I told her about the poem and asked if she wanted me to
share it. "Yes," she replied, "If it is brief, for my energy is too
low to concentrate long." I read it to her. "Thank you. Thank you,
Laura," were her words and we hung up.

Two days later, I learned Virginia had stopped taking the cleansing medicines, she had stopped vomiting, which she had been doing
for several days. She was resting quietly. I knew it was time for me
to go.

When she saw me at her bedroom door, she said, "Come in. I
want to feel your energy." She signaled a chair by her side with her
eyes, and I sat down. We were silent, eyes closed, for ten to fifteen
minutes. During that time, two or three other people who were in
the room left.

Virginia took her hand out from under the covers and I took that
as a signal to hold her hand. I did, and we were silent another ten
minutes or so. Her eyes closed again. The setting sun and the lovely

evening hues coming into the soft room from the glass wall seemed to hold us.

"What would you say, Laura, if I said I want to make my transition now?"

Quiet again. So profound words, so profound a moment. We sat quietly again for a couple of minutes. I found myself responding, "Virginia, if that is what you feel is right for you, I will help you."

She opened her eyes and the glowing smile I had seen so often on her face was there. Her eyes sparkled. "I am 72, I have lived a good life." We looked into each other's eyes for a time.

After a time, Virginia asked, "Laura, would you give me a massage? Turn up the music loudly." I was delighted to share this ritual with her at this time. It was one we had experienced many times, and it seemed so perfect now. I don't know what classical music was playing, but the room filled with soft, strong energy. Whenever our eyes would meet her glowing smile would be there. Once she whispered, "It's so right, it's so right . . . "

"I know, Virginia, it is so right."

Ecstasy was in the air . . . it radiated around and in us. We were celebrating her decision to die!! Weird though it may sound, it was a truly ecstatic experience.

After about an hour, I leaned over to Virginia and asked, "How do you feel now about your decision?"

Softly and assuredly came back, "It is the only thing that gives me peace."

We were quiet as the last of evening died into the dark of night. In the background was the mumble and bustle of the other people who were in the house as they were tending to phone calls, visiting, preparing food. I asked, "What shall I say when I leave the room and meet the others here?"

"Nothing," she replied, "Say nothing. Not yet."

She needed time with her decision. Time to feel if it were really right. She needed full freedom to be with it . . . I left the room and said nothing.

For the first shift of the night, I was on call to Virginia. She would ring her bell often for help. The first two or three times the requests were for the mechanics of life, but the feeling was more. The fourth time, I asked, "Virginia, would you like me to sleep in here?"

"Oh yes, that would be good." Her restlessness died down for awhile and she slept. Someone awakened me about 3:00 a.m. to relieve my duty. Another loving friend came in and sat beside her.

The next morning Virginia looked tired and tense. She asked that I tell others now of her decision. I left her for an hour and shared with the four women who were there. When I returned to Virginia she was in more motion than before but silent. Then she lifted her head and looked straight into my eyes with an intense look of panic on her face. "Laura, I am so afraid!" Overwhelmed with her intense feeling, I didn't know what to say and finally blurted out, "What shall we do about your fear, Virginia?" She didn't know, of course. If she had known, she wouldn't have asked the question! I felt lost, overwhelmed yet focused and searching . . . this was the first very difficult task in my commitment to help her with her decision. I went into a room away from others in the house, determined to sit there until I had something to say to her.

Time passed — maybe an hour or so — before I found myself running back into her room without the words of my response yet formed, but I knew they were there. "About your fear, Virginia, this is what we do. We know you are going to die."

"Yes," she said. "Next Sunday." (This was Sunday.)

"We set that aside over here," I motioned to the right of me as far as my arm could go. "That is a given," and paused to see her agreement. "Now, we focus on each moment between now and then, we focus deeply, and we do in each moment exactly what needs to be done in the most perfect way that we can." So simple, but what relief this brought to us.

Virginia slept several hours and those of us in the household began from a meditative stance to try to anticipate what needed to be done and how it might be done just right.

Virginia took charge of her dying just as she took charge of her living. Later that day, when I asked "What needs to be done now?" She replied, "Call my brother and his wife, and my daughters."

"And what about your sister," I asked, knowing Virginia had not seen her for some years. Surprised at herself, she exclaimed, "Oh, I forgot about her." Her hearing was fading, and as she would have done for me, I put my face to hers and said in a loud voice, "Now, that you remember, what shall we do?" "Call her too," she sighed. So the journey was begun of doing each thing in its proper way and in its proper time.

Her brother arrived with his wife and grandson. In his great love for Virginia, her brother exclaimed, "Ginny, what are you doing? You can't give up on life. You have always been a fighter."

She opened her eyes, looked him right in the eye, and exclaimed, "Russell, you just don't understand! I am not giving up on life. I am following my peace."

After trying to persuade her to go for chemotherapy, etc., and meeting only her closed eyes, his grandson of 19 put his arm around his shoulder and said, "Granddad, if Aunt Ginny wants to die, let's just let her," and they left the room.

I commented, "Your brother is having a hard time with your decision."

"Of course he is. So am I."

During periodic talks the next few days Virginia actively worked out more details of her dying, calling in people she needed to talk with to find the right details for her. "I want to be fully conscious as long as I can. I want to be with this process. Keep the pain meds as low as possible." Another time . . . "everyone has to die some-time — no one gets out of this world alive." She had calls from Moscow, Israel, South America, Sweden, all of Europe, all over this country. Mail piled high. She screened carefully and felt concerned that we carefully convey hers was not a message of rejection but of limits of time that must be preserved for her inner process. Times like this are timeless, days seemed like weeks.

On September 5th, five days before she died, Virginia dictated the following message:

> To all my friends, colleagues and family:
> I send you love.
> Please support me in my passage to a new life.
> I have no other way to thank you than this.
> You have all played a significant part in my development of loving.
> As a result, my life has been rich and full, so I leave feeling very grateful.
>
> Virginia

Now, Virginia talked less, slept more. Her sentences were often partial ones. She was considering rituals and ceremonies for her death. One morning she woke alert and instructed us to have flowers and music and sit together in her living room after she died. Then she slept heavily again. In another brief moment of her awake state to this world, she asked that all the people in the house be called into her room and ten or so people came in. She instructed each to go around the house and choose a piece of art or sculpture as their own, and to return to her and tell her why they had chosen that one. The ritual seemed so satisfying to her.

Virginia requested that music — often meditative music — be played into the earphone set she wore. She liked *The Course in Miracles* read to her. She slept more and deeper.

She began to use the phrase, "I am going home, wish me well on my journey." Visions came to her . . . one was of crossing a river and seeing others who had died on the other side reaching for her. The house became like a sanctuary. We looked in each moment for guidance for the next. There was more silence. We moved in quiet rhythms together. A nurse was always there. A special friend was especially present to Virginia for each of three shifts of the day.

On Thursday morning, Virginia asked that we contact about 12 close friends whom she felt could help to "wish me home" to come to her on Friday. They all did. Before they began to arrive, Virginia had slipped into a deep coma from which she never awoke. She died on Saturday at 5:10 p.m., September 10.

In the 24 hours before her death, her home was like a holy mosque, church, synagogue, all in one — a place of deep meditation. The California sun shone brightly. Her family and friends came together to talk quietly in the lovely yard, to sit in meditation and to share together. We were all wishing her home. On Saturday morning before entering her room we could see the pumps of the oxygen she was taking was still in operation. Sighs came, sighs of despair, as that meant Virginia has not yet made it out of her body. We were indeed wishing her home. Later that day the family decided to stop the oxygen.

When she did breathe a last gentle breath, with no struggle, we gathered around her bed holding hands. The ecstatic feeling was there again though tainted with deep loss. She made it out of her body!

Almost without thought, ritualistic behavior fell in line. Jonathan, one of her doctors, who is Jewish, conducted the last ceremony in his tradition of breaking the glass as a symbol of transition. We spoke quietly to her. Some sang.

As it was right, we left the room and tended to the business of calling people, making arrangements with the crematory she had chosen, getting information to the newspapers. When the crematory came, we quietly walked behind as they carried her still, peaceful, beautiful body. We scattered rose petals over her cover and on the ground. It was the glow of evening time again.

In her dying days, Virginia was fortunate to have minimal pain, or at least pain that could be controlled, and an illness that did not cloud her mind. She provided a strong model of a dying process for us, and one that she wanted to share with the world.

She taught me that death is like birth. A barrier had been there in my mind . . . a barrier to the knowledge that there is no end. It faded and has remained faded. With this absence there is a deeper sense of freedom. Life and death seem a circle and passage either way seems natural and full. "Thank you, Virginia."

As a part of her obituary, Jean Houston wrote of Virginia:

> Virginia was one of the greatest geniuses of our time. She brought the field of family therapy to a new level. She anticipated a need for and created patterns for a deep healing in the 21st century for cultures and nations as well as individuals and families. Rarely in one human being is so much heart matched with so much mindfulness.

Virginia Satir Bibliography

Compiled by Lynne M. Azpeitia

Andreas, S. (1989, Jan./Feb.). The true genius of Virginia Satir. *The Family Therapy Networker*, pp. 51-56 & 78-80.

Bandler, R., Grinder, J., & Satir, V. (1976). *Changing with families*. Palo Alto, CA: Science and Behavior Books.

Banmen, J. (1986, Dec.). Virginia Satir's family therapy model. *Individual Psychology Journal of Adlerian Theory, Research and Practice, 42*(4), 480-492.

Banmen, J., & Gerber, J. (Eds.). (1985). *Virginia Satir's meditations and inspirations*. Berkeley, CA: Celestial Art.

Bitter, J. R. (1988, March). Family mapping and family constellation: Satir in Adlerian context. *Individual Psychology Journal of Adlerian Theory, Research and Practice, 44*(1), 106-111.

Braverman, S. (1986, Summer). Heinz Kohut and Virginia Satir: Strange bedfellows? *Contemporary Family Therapy: An International Journal, 8*(2), 101-110.

Brothers, B. J. (1987). Independence *avoids* intimacy: Avoidance of intimacy kills. *Voices: The Art and Science of Psychotherapy, 23*(1), 10-23.

Brothers, B. J. (1988). Remorse and regeneration. *Psychotherapy Patient, 5*(1-2), 47-62.

Brothers, B. J. (1988). The cancer patient is the self-contained patient. *Psychotherapy Patient, 4*(3-4), 227-241.

Brothers, B. J. (1990). Self-esteem and congruent communication: Virginia Satir's road to integration. *Advanced Development, 2*, 23-34.

Lynne M. Azpeitia, MA, member, Virginia Satir's Avanta Network, is Professor of Family Therapy and Director of Interns, California Family Study Center, 5433 Laurel Canyon Blvd., North Hollywood, CA 91607.

Corrales, R. G. (1989, Jan./Feb.). Drawing out the best. *The Family Therapy Networker*, pp. 45-49.

Duhl, B.S. (1989). Virginia Satir: In memoriam. *Journal of Marital and Family Therapy*, *15*(2), 109-110.

Ebert, B. (1978). Homeostasis. *Family Therapy*, *5*(2), 171-175.

Englander, G. P., Elconin, J., & Satir, V. (1986, Summer). Assertive/leveling communication and empathy in adolescent drug abuse prevention. *Journal of Primary Prevention*, *6*(4), 231-243.

Fishman, H. C. (Ed.). (1986). *Evolving models for family change: A volume in honor of Salvador Minuchin.* New York: The Guilford Press.

Gordon, L., Duhl, B. S., Duhl, F. J., McGoldrick, M., Pittman, F., & Baldwin, M. (1989, Jan./Feb.). Remembering Virginia. *The Family Therapy Networker*, pp. 27-35.

Gottfarb, L. (1985). Virginia Satir still going strong. (From the International Human Learning Resources Network's international conference in Sveti Stefan, Yugoslavia, September 1985.) *Psykisk-Halsa*, *26*(4), 218-219.

Green, R. G., & Kolevzon, M. S. (1984, Oct.). Characteristics of healthy families. *Elementary School Guidance and Counseling*, *19*(1), 9-18.

Jackson, D., & Satir, V. (1961). A review of psychiatric development in family diagnosis and family therapy. In N., Ackerman, F. Beatman, & S. Sherman (Eds.), *Exploring the base for family therapy.* New York: Family Service Association of America.

Kramer, S. Z. (1988, Nov./Dec.). In memory of Virginia Satir. *The California Therapist*, pp. 3-4.

Kramer, S. Z. (1988, Dec.). Memories are made of this. *AHP Perspective*, pp. 4-11.

Kramer, S. Z. (1989, Winter). In memory of Virginia Satir. *AFTA Newsletter*, pp. 3-8.

Middelberg, C. V., & Gross, S. J. (1979). Families' affective rules and their relationship to the families' adjustment. *American Journal of Family Therapy*, *7*(2), 37-45.

Mulholland, R. (1985, Nov.). Linking theoretical concepts and models in social work assessment. *Journal of Social Work Practice*, *2*(1), 4-23.

Nerin, W. F. (1989, March/April). Satir is very learnable: Trainees lead changes in family reconstruction. *AAMFT Family Therapy News*, p. 3.

Nerin, W. F. (1989, Jan./Feb.). You can go home again. *The Family Therapy Networker*, pp. 54-55.

Oz, S. (1988, Fall). A modified "parts party" for couples work. *Contemporary Family Therapy: An International Journal*, *10*(3), 183-193.

Satir, V. (1975, Feb.). Family life education: A perspective on the educator. *Small Group Behavior*, *6*(1), 3-10.

Satir, V. (1983). (1967). (1964). *Conjoint family therapy*. Palo Alto, CA: Science and Behavior Books.

Satir, V. (1972). *Peoplemaking*. Palo Alto, CA: Science and Behavior Books.

Satir, V. (1975). *Self-esteem*. Millbrae, CA: Celestial Arts.

Satir, V. (1976). *Making contact*. Millbrae, CA: Celestial Arts.

Satir, V. (1978). *Your many faces*. Millbrae, CA: Celestial Arts.

Satir, V. (1987, Spring). The therapist story. (Special issue: The use of self in therapy.) *Journal of Psychotherapy and the Family*, *3*(1), 17-25.

Satir, V. (1988). *The new peoplemaking*. Mountain View, CA: Science and Behavior Books, Inc.

Satir, V. (Presenter). *Blended family with a troubled boy (family interview)* (videocassette). Kansas City, MO: Golden Triad Films.

Satir, V. (Presenter). *Rocks and flowers* (videocassette). Kansas City, MO: Golden Triad Films.

Satir, V. (Presenter). *A family at the point of growth* (videocassette). Kansas City, MO: Golden Triad Films.

Satir, V. (Presenter). *A step along the way* (videocassette). Kansas City, MO: Golden Triad Films.

Satir, V. (Presenter). *The Essence of Change* (videocassette). Kansas City, MO: Golden Triad Films.

Satir, V. (Presenter). *The peoplemaking series: The process of change* (videocassette). Paradise, CA: Peoplemaking.

Satir, V. (Presenter). *The peoplemaking series: Virginia Satir: Philosophy and teachings* (videocassette). Paradise, CA: Peoplemaking.

Satir, V. (Presenter). *The peoplemaking series: Promise and delivery* (videocassette). Paradise, CA: Peoplemaking.

Satir, V. (Presenter). *The peoplemaking series: Virginia Satir's meditations* (videocassette). Paradise, CA: Peoplemaking.

Satir, V. (Presenter). *The peoplemaking series: The Chico tapes* (videocassettes). Paradise, CA: Peoplemaking.

Satir, V. (Presenter). *The peoplemaking series: The culminating sessions of the Chico tapes* (videocassette). Paradise, CA: Peoplemaking.

Satir, V., Bitter, J. R., & Krestensen, K. K. (1988, Nov.). Family reconstruction: The family within a group experience. (Special issue: The interface of group work and family therapy: Implications for practice.) *Journal for Specialists in Group Work*, *13*(4), 200-208.

Satir, V., Stachowiak, J., & Taschman, H. (1977). *Helping families to change*. New York: Aronson.

Satir, V., & Baldwin, M. (1983). *Satir step by step*. Palo Alto, CA: Science and Behavior Books.

Satir, V. (1982). The therapist and family therapy: Process Model. In A. Horne & M. Ohlsen (Eds.), *Family counseling and therapy*. Itasca, IL: F.E. Peacock Publishers, Inc.

Satir, V. (1967). A family of Angels. In J. Haley & L. Hoffman, *Techniques of Family*. New York: Basic Books.

Satir, V. (1977). Personal growth and the family. *Synthesis*, *3 & 4*, pp. 172-193.

Schwab, J., Baldwin, M., Gerber, J., Gomori, M., & Satir, V. (1989). *The Satir approach to communication* (A workshop manual). Palo Alto, CA: Science and Behavior Books.

Simon, R. (1985, Winter). Life reaching out to life: A conversation with Virginia Satir. *The Common Boundary*, pp. 1-12.

Simon, R. (1989, Jan./Feb.). Reaching out to life. *The Family Therapy Networker*. pp. 37-43.

Textor, P. M. (1989, Jan.). Family Therapy: Schoolism and eclecticism. *Indian Journal of Psychological Medicine*, *12*(1), 9-12.

Woods, M. D., & Martin, D. (1984, Winter). The work of Virginia Satir: Understanding her theory and technique. *American Journal of Family Therapy*, *12*(4), 3-11.

Zahnd, W.F. (1987). *Crested Butte temperature reading chart*. Paradise, CA: Author.

Index

Affect
  Satir on, 5
  shame as, 144-146,147,149,151
Ahimsa, 4,9
American Association of Marriage
    and Family Therapy, 8
Andersen, Leo, 169
Anger, 63
Archetypes, Jungian theory of, 67
Autonomy, in marital relationship,
    59,60,70,73,74,75,76
Avanta Conference, 180
Avanta Process Communities, 14

Baldwin, Michele, 2,160
Barnes, Craig, 181
Bateson, Gregory, 122
Bateson, Mary Catherine, 181
Breakthrough, 181
Burnett, M'Lou, 181

Center of Therapeutic
    Communication, 169
Chalice and the Blade (Eisler), 181
Change, process of, 119-142
  components, 122-137
    chaos, 129-134,136,137,138
    new status quo, 135,136,137,
      138
    practice, 134-135,136,137,138
    resistance, 127-129,136,137,
      138
    status quo, 123-127,129,131,
      135,137,138
  during life cycle, 137-139
  philosophical basis, 120-122
  Satir's approach to, 122-123,161
  theoretical basis, 120-122
  world peace and, 139-141

Chaos, in change process, 129-134,
    136,137,138
Character, development of, 22
Children
  coping strategies, 30-31,47-48
  dyadic relationships, 31-33
  shame, 144,145-146,147,150-153
Communication. *See also*
    Temperature Reading
  congruent, 7,13-16
    in change process, 131-132
    training exercises for, 36
  dysfunctional, 34-35
  as family therapy goal, 169
  free, 25
  importance, 84
  incongruent, 14,15-19
    being super-irrelevant, 18
    being super-reasonable, 18
    blaming, 16-18
    physical implications, 18-19
    placating, 16
  patterns, 12
  Satir's style of, 160-161
  within triad, 33,34-35
Competence, development of, 59,70
Conflict, intrapsychic, 22-23
Congruence, 11,161
  in communication, 7,13-16
    in change process, 131-132
    definition, 15
    training exercises for, 36
  definition, 14,15
  in Family Reconstruction, 61
  interpersonal, 14
  intrapersonal, 14
  self-esteem and, 5-6
  truth and, 19-20
Connectedness, 7,11-20

Made in the USA
Columbia, SC
28 December 2023

29577922R00115